I0764240

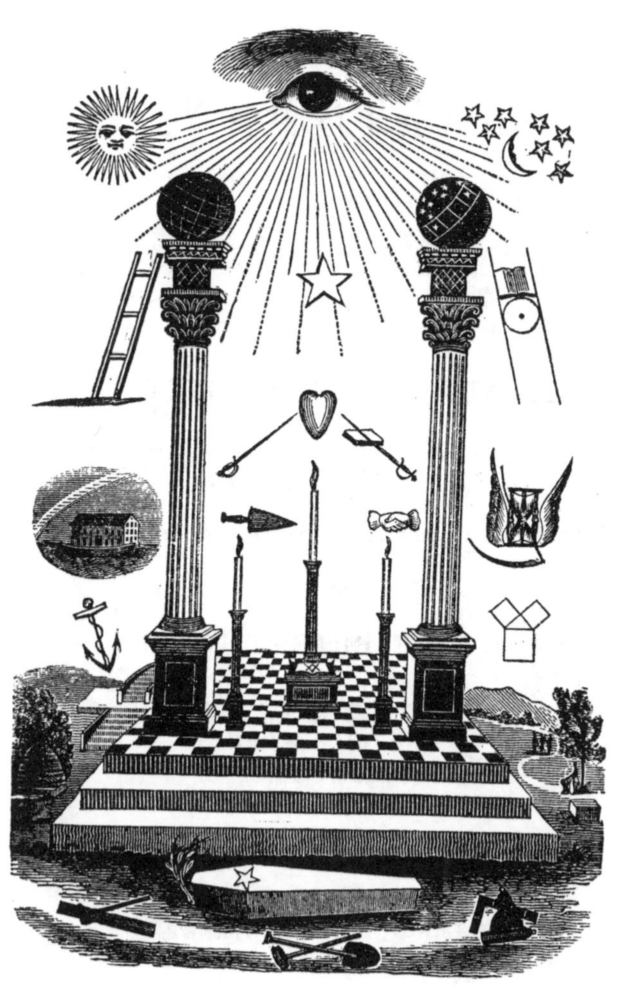

THE

CRAFTSMAN,

AND

FREEMASON'S GUIDE;

CONTAINING A DELINEATION OF THE

RITUALS OF FREEMASONRY,

WITH THE EMBLEMS AND EXPLANATIONS SO ARRANGED AS GREATLY TO FACILITATE IN ACQUIRING A KNOWLEDGE OF THE RITES AND CEREMONIES OF THE SEVERAL DEGREES, FROM

ENTERED APPRENTICE TO THAT OF SELECT MASTER,

AND THE

ORDER OF PRIESTHOOD.

COMPILED AND ARRANGED FROM WEBB, AND OTHER STANDARD AUTHORS:
BY CORNELIUS MOORE,
Past Master of Lafayette Lodge, No. 79, and Editor of the Masonic Review, Cincinnati.

FOURTH EDITION.

CINCINNATI:
JACOB ERNST, 183 MAIN STREET,
PHILADELPHIA: E. H. BUTLER & CO., 23 MINOR ST.
1851.

CIRCLEVILLE, March 12th, 1846.

Having examined the manuscript pages of a work prepared by Bro. CORNELIUS MOORE, entitled, "THE CRAFTSMAN, AND FREEMASON'S GUIDE," I have no hesitation in commending it to the favorable consideration of the fraternity in Ohio, and elsewhere, as a useful, convenient, and compendious Text-Book, for the use of Lodges and private brethren. It is a judicious compilation from standard masonic authors; and in point of the arrangement of its matter, is preferable in my estimation, to any work of the kind which has fallen under my observation. Especially in the hands of those upon whom devolve the active duties of the Lodge and Chapter, it will be found a ready and acceptable Manual of masonry. By the exclusion from its pages of much that is interesting chiefly to those of far-reaching curiosity—while all is retained that is necessary for the exemplification of our principles, or to aid in the practice of our rites—the work is brought within a convenient compass, and is afforded at so low a price as to place it within the reach of every brother.

W. B. THRALL,
Grand Master of the Grand Lodge of Ohio.

We entirely concur in the above.

SAMUEL REED,
Grand Lecturer.

ROBERT PUNSHON,
G. Chaplain of the G. G. R. A. Chapter of the U. S.

To the Officers and Members of the Grand Lodge of the Most Ancient and Honorable Fraternity of Free and Accepted Masons of the State of Ohio:

BRETHREN—The high regard I entertain for you, individually and collectively, as Men and as Masons, and the valuable assistance rendered me in the preparation of the following Work by the M. W. Grand Master, and Grand Lecturer, have induced me, as a testimonial of my respect and gratitude, to dedicate to you this volume. Hoping that it may be found worthy of your approbation, and prove a benefit to our Ancient Fraternity every where,

I am, respectfully,

And Fraternally,

Yours,

C. MOORE.

PREFACE TO THE FIRST EDITION.

WE have no apology to make in presenting the following compilation to the Masonic Fraternity. All agree that some work of the kind is needed at the present time. The great and constantly increasing accessions to our Order in the West, and the renewed attentions to our peculiar rites and ceremonies, have created a demand for a *practical* book. Webb's Monitor, which by many was considered the best of its kind, has long been out of print, and its truly excellent author sleeps in peace with his Fathers.

One thing to be especially guarded against at the present time, is a *variance* in the practice of our rites, and the work of our Lodges and Chapters. Next to guarding the principles which impart vitality to our institution, and preserving unchanged the ancient landmarks of our Order, it is important to attain and preserve *uniformity* in the mode of discharging the duties of the Lodge-room. It was deemed by many that a book in which our emblems should be placed in juxtaposition with their explanations, and so arranged in the work itself as to serve as a guide to the memory, would aid in obtaining and perpetuating those desirable results. Still no one appeared to undertake the task; and the Compiler of this book, distrusting his own qualifications, would have long hesitated, had not an esteemed friend, Brother SAMUEL REED, the excellent and indefatigable

Grand Lecturer of the Grand Lodge and Grand Chapter of Ohio, expressed his willingness to aid in the undertaking. With this encouragement the Compiler commenced his labor, and devoted several months of close application to it, resorting for aid to the work of every approved masonic author, from Preston down, to which he could gain access.

After going through and arranging the whole to the close of the Royal Arch degree, he submitted the result of his labors to the examination of Bro. REED, who made such alterations and corrections, as he deemed proper, in order that it might conform strictly to the mode of work in the several degrees as taught by him, and approved by the Grand Lodge, Grand Chapter, and Grand Council of Ohio.

The manuscript was subsequently placed in the hands of WILLIAM B. THRALL, Esq., the Grand Master of the Grand Lodge of Ohio —"a workman that needeth not to be ashamed,"—and also submitted to our venerable Companion, Rev. ROBERT PUNSHON, of this city, both of whom were pleased to give it the sanction of their approbation. It is proper here to say, that the part which treats of the Order of Priesthood, was arranged *exclusively* by Brother REED, as the Compiler has not had the honor of that Order.

The Compiler does not suppose that the work is perfect; but he believes it will render efficient aid in acquiring a correct knowledge of our rites, and in discharging the duties of our Lodge and Chapter rooms.

He knows that it is an easy matter for the critical and conceited to find fault—far easier than to produce a work of this kind *without faults.* Such as it is, however, he submits to his Masonic Brethren. COMPILER.

NOTE TO THE STEREOTYPE EDITION.

THE demand for this work having been such as to require several large editions in a few years, the publisher has been induced to stereotype it; and in order that it may be as perfect as possible, the undersigned has called to his aid Brother SAMUEL REED, Past Grand Lecturer of the Grand Lodge of Ohio, at whose instance some useful improvements have been made. The whole work has been re-examined, and a few errors that have heretofore escaped the Compiler's notice, have been corrected. The *arrangement* remains precisely the same as in former editions. Some additional illustrations have been added, and others have been re-engraved and much improved. It is hoped that in its present matured condition it will fully meet the wants of those for whom it was originally compiled and arranged.

As it has already received the approval of several Grand Lodges, and many distinguished Masons in different States, the undersigned trusts it may continue to deserve the patronage of the workmen in every apartment of our mystic building.

C. MOORE.

CINCINNATI, OHIO, *October*, 1850.

INDEX.

PART FIRST.

CHAPTER I.

CHAPTER II.

CHAPTER III.

CHAPTER IV.

CHAPTER V.

CHAPTER VI.

PART SECOND.

CHAPTER I.

CHAPTER II.

PART THIRD.

PART FOURTH.

THE CRAFTSMAN.

PART FIRST.

CHAPTER I.

GENERAL REMARKS.

MASONRY is an art equally useful and extensive. In every part there is a mystery which requires a gradual progression of knowledge to arrive at any degree of perfection in it. Without much instruction, and more exercise, no man can be skilful in any art: in like manner, without an assiduous application to the various subjects treated of in the different lectures of Masonry, no person can be sufficiently acquainted with its true value.

It must not, however, be inferred from this remark, that persons who labor under the disadvantages of a limited education, or whose condition in life requires a more intense application to business or study, are to be discouraged in their endeavors to gain a knowledge of Masonry.

To qualify an individual to enjoy the benefit of the society at large, or to partake of its privileges, it is not absolutely necessary that he should be acquainted with all the intricate parts of the science. These are only intended for the diligent and assiduous Mason, who may have leisure and opportunity to indulge in such pursuits.

Though some are more able than others, some more eminent, some more useful, yet all, in their different spheres, may prove advantageous to the community. As the nature of every man's profession will not admit of that leisure which is necessary to qualify him to become an expert Mason, it is highly proper that the official duties of a Lodge should be executed by persons whose education and situation in life enable them to become adepts; as it must be allowed that all who accept offices and exercise authority should be properly qualified to discharge the task assigned them, with honor to themselves and credit to their respective stations.

CHAPTER II.

THE CEREMONY OF OPENING AND CLOSING THE LODGE.

In all regular assemblies of men who are convened for wise and useful purposes, the commencement and conclusion of business are accompanied with some form. In every country the practice prevails, and is deemed essential. From the most remote periods of antiquity it may be traced, and the refined improvements of modern times have not totally abolished it.

Ceremonies, when simply considered, it is true, are of but little value; but their effects are sometimes important. When they impress awe and reverence on the mind, and engage the attention to solemn rites by external attraction, they are interesting objects. These purposes are effected by judicious ceremonies, when regularly conducted and properly arranged. On this ground they have received the sanction of the wisest men in all ages, and consequently could not escape the notice of Masons. To begin well, is the most likely means to end well: and it is judiciously remarked, that when order and method are neglected at the beginning, they will be seldom found to take place at the end.

The importance of performing the ceremony of opening and closing a Lodge with solemnity and decorum, is therefore universally admitted among Masons; and though the mode in some Lodges may vary, and in every *degree must* vary, still an uniformity in the general practice prevails in every Lodge; and the variation (if any) is solely occasioned by a want of method, which a little application might easily remove.

To conduct this ceremony with propriety, ought to be the particular study of every Mason; especially of those who have the honor to rule in our assemblies. To persons who are thus dignified, every eye is naturally directed for propriety of conduct and behaviour; and from them, other brethren who are less informed, will naturally expect an example worthy of imitation.

From a share in this ceremony no Mason can be exempted. It is a general concern, in which all must assist. This is the first request of the Master and the prelude to all business. No sooner has it been signified, than every officer repairs to his station, and the brethren rank according to their degrees. The business of the meeting becomes the sole object of attention, and the mind is insensibly drawn from those indiscriminate subjects of conversation, which are apt to intrude on our less serious moments.

This effect accomplished, our care is directed to the external avenues of the Lodge; and the proper officers, whose province it is to discharge that duty, execute their trust with fidelity, and by certain mystic forms, of no recent date, intimate that we may safely proceed. To detect imposters among ourselves, an adherence to order in the character of Masons ensues, and the Lodge is opened in solemn form.

At opening the Lodge, two purposes are wisely effected: the Master is reminded of the dignity of his character, and the brethren of the homage and veneration due from them in their respective stations. These are not the only advantages resulting from a due observance of this ceremony; a reverential awe for the Deity is inculcated, and the eye fixed on that object, from whose radiant beams only, light can be derived.

Here we are taught to adore the God of Heaven, and to supplicate his blessing on our well meant endeavors. The Master assumes his government in due form, and under him his Wardens, who accept their trust, after the customary salutations. The brethren then, with one accord, unite in duty and respect, and the ceremony concludes.

At closing the Lodge a similar form is used. Here the less important duties of Masonry are not passed over unobserved. The necessary degree of subordination in the government of a Lodge is peculiarly marked, while the proper tribute of gratitude is offered up to the beneficent Author of life, and his blessing invoked upon the whole fraternity. Each brother faithfully locks up the treasure he has acquired, in his own secret repository; and, pleased with his reward, retires to enjoy and disseminate among the private circle of his brethren, the fruits of his labor and industry in the Lodge.

These are faint outlines of a ceremony which universally prevails among Masons in every country, and distinguishes all their meetings. It is arranged as a general section in every degree, and takes the lead in all our illustrations.

CHARGE USED AT OPENING A LODGE.

Behold! how good and how pleasant it is for brethren to dwell together in unity!

It is like the precious ointment upon the head, that ran down upon the beard, even Aaron's beard, that went down to the skirts of his garments;

As the dew of Hermon, and as the dew that descended upon the mountains of Zion; for there the Lord commanded the blessing, even life forever more.

A PRAYER USED AT CLOSING A LODGE.

May the blessing of Heaven rest upon us, and all regular Masons: may brotherly love prevail, and every moral and social virtue cement us. Amen.

[NOTE.—*If a clergyman be present, he may be requested by the Master to lead in the devotion at opening and closing.*]

CHARGE AT CLOSING A LODGE.

BRETHREN:—You are now about to quit this sacred retreat of *friendship* and *virtue,* to mix again with the world. Amidst its concerns and temptations, forget not the duties you have heard so frequently inculcated and so forcibly recommended in this Lodge. Be diligent, prudent, temperate, discreet. Remember that you have promised to befriend and relieve every brother who shall need your assistance: you have promised to remind him, in the most friendly manner, of his errors; and if possible, aid him in a reformation. These generous principles are to extend further. Every human being has a claim upon your kind offices. Do good unto all. Remember it more "especially to the household of the faithful."

Finally, brethren, be ye all of one mind, live in peace, and may the God of love and peace delight to dwell with and bless you.

CHAPTER III.

INSTRUCTIONS TO A PERSON WISHING TO BECOME A MASON.

No person can become a Mason, consistently with the ancient and salutary usages of our order, unless he be free born, and, at least twenty-one years of age; of a good moral character; temperate, industrious, charitable, and possessed of public spirit and the social virtues. He must be of sufficient natural endowments to be respectable, and must have, entire, all the faculties and senses of a *man*. He must also have an estate, office, trade, occupation, or some visible means of acquiring an honest livelihood, as becomes the members of this ancient and honorable fraternity. In short, he must have a sound head and a good heart, and be exempt from all those ill qualities and vices which bring dishonor to the craft.

A person possessing the foregoing qualifications must be proposed, at his own voluntary request, by a friend or acquaintance belonging to the Lodge of which he wishes to become a member, at least one meeting previous to the time of initiation.

All applications for admission should be made in writing, in the following form:

"*To the Worshipful Master, Wardens and Brethren of —— Lodge, No. —, of Free and Accepted Masons:*

The petition of the subscriber respectfully sheweth, that, entertaining a favorable opinion of your ancient institution, he is desirous of being admitted a member thereof, if found worthy.

His place of residence is ———, his age —— years, his occupation ———.

Recommended by } (*Signed*)
A. B."

Before admission, the candidate must assent to the following interrogatories:

"Do you seriously declare, upon your honor, that unbiassed by friends, and uninfluenced by mercenary motives, you freely and voluntarily offer yourself a candidate for the mysteries of Masonry?

"Do you seriously declare, upon your honor, that you are prompted to solicit the privileges of Masonry by a favorable opinion of the institution, a desire for knowledge, and a sincere wish of being serviceable to your fellow creatures?

"Do you seriously declare, upon your honor, that you will conform to all the ancient established usages of the order?"

If there remain no objection, the candidate is introduced in due form. But he has a right, previous to presenting himself, to desire his friend to show him the warrant or dispensation by which the Lodge is held; which, if genuine, he will find to be an instrument written or printed upon paper or parchment, signed by some Grand Master or his Deputy, the Grand Wardens and Secretary, and sealed with the Grand Lodge Seal.

He may also request the perusal of the By-laws, and has a right to examine a complete list of the members, to learn whether the Lodge contains any member with whom he cannot consistently and cordially associate.

Should the candidate find the charter to be genuine, the by-laws salutary, and such as he can cheerfully observe; and should he be pleased with all the brethren of the Lodge, his wish to proceed is reported to the Master, who makes it known to the Lodge.

CHAPTER IV.

ENTERED APPRENTICE'S DEGREE.

THE first lecture of Masonry is divided into three sections, and each section into several clauses. Virtue is painted in the most beautiful colors, and the duties of morality are enforced. In it we are taught various useful lessons, to prepare the mind for a regular advancement in the principles of knowledge and philosophy. These are imprinted on the mind by lively and sensible hieroglyphical figures, which are here explained, and which have a moral tendency, and inculcate the practice of virtue.

Section First.

This part of the lecture of an Entered Apprentice unfolds our *object* in visiting the hall of Masonry; develops the justice of our *pretensions* to the privileges of the order; illustrates the *manner* of our reception within the threshhold of a Lodge; reminds us of our *dependence* on the supporting hand of Deity; exhibits the *pledge* of our fidelity, secrecy, and conformity to immemorial masonic customs; opens our eyes to the *light* of knowledge; presents to our hearts the lovely purity of *innocence;* draws upon our *affections* by the silken cord of charity; and speculatively explains the *implements* of the degree.

A prayer used at the initiation of a candidate.

Vouchsafe thine aid, Almighty Father of the Universe, to this our present convention; and grant that this candidate for Masonry may dedicate and devote his life to thy service, and become a true and faithful brother among us! Endow him with a competency of thy divine wisdom, that, by the secrets of our art, he may be better enabled to display the beauties of *brotherly love, relief*, and *truth*, to the honor of thy holy name. Amen.

Or this,

O thou supreme Author of our being and lover of our souls;—thou who art every where present, and knowest the thoughts and intentions of our hearts; bless us, we pray thee, in our endeavors to do good, and spread peace and concord and unity among our fellow men. May this our friend, who is now to become our brother, devote his life to thy service and his talents to thy glory. May he be endowed with wisdom to direct him in all his ways, strength to support him in all his difficulties, and the beauty of morality and virtue to adorn his life. May he set Thee constantly before his eyes, and seek thy approbation as his greatest treasure. May he become enlightened in the knowledge of divine things, and be induced to love Thee from thy manifest love to him. And may he and we regulate our actions by the light of thy revealed truth, and so construct our spiritual edifice, that when done laboring as apprentices in this lower temple, we may be raised to the sublime employments of the upper sanctuary—in that temple not made with hands, eternal in the heavens, whose builder and maker is God. Amen.

Behold! how good and how pleasant it is for brethren to dwell together in unity! &c.

Toward the close of the section is explained that

peculiar ensign of masonry, the *lamb-skin* or *white apron*, which is an emblem of innocence and the badge of a Mason; more ancient than the golden fleece, or Roman eagle; and when worthily worn, more honorable than the star and garter, or any other order that could be conferred upon the candidate at that or any future period. It has been worn by kings, princes, and potentates of the earth, who have never been ashamed to wear it, and which every one ought to wear with equal pleasure to himself and honor to the fraternity.

This section closes with an explanation of the *working tools* of an Entered Apprentice, which are the *twenty-four inch gauge* and the *common gavel.*

The *twenty-four inch gauge* is an instrument made use of by operative masons, to measure and lay out their work; but we, as free and accepted Masons, are taught to make use of it for the more noble and glorious purpose of dividing our time. It being divided into twenty-four equal parts is emblematical of the twenty-four hours of the day, which we are taught to divide into *three* parts, whereby we find a portion for the service of God and the relief of a distressed worthy brother; a portion for our usual avocations, and a portion for refreshment and sleep.

The *common gavel* is an instrument made use of by operative masons, to break off the superfluous corners of rough stones, the better to fit them for the builder's use; but we, as free and accepted Masons, are taught to make use of it for the more noble and glorious purpose of divesting our minds and consciences of all the vices and superfluities of life; thereby fitting us, as living stones, for that spiritual building, that house not made with hands, eternal in the heavens.

Section Second.

The second section rationally accounts for the ceremony of initiating a candidate into our ancient institution.

* * * * * * *

Every candidate, at his initiation, is presented with a *lamb-skin* or *white apron*.

The *Lamb* has, in all ages, been deemed an emblem of *innocence;* he, therefore, who wears the lamb-skin as a badge of Masonry, is thereby continually reminded of that purity of life and conduct, which is essentially necessary to his gaining admission into the Celestial Lodge above, where the Supreme Architect of the Universe presides. * * * * * * *

Section Third.

This section explains what constitutes a Lodge, and teaches us to perform with propriety, the duties of our respective stations. Here likewise, we receive instruction relative to the *form*, *supports*, *covering*, *furniture*, *ornaments*, *lights* and *jewels* of a Lodge; how it should be *situated*, and to whom *dedicated*.

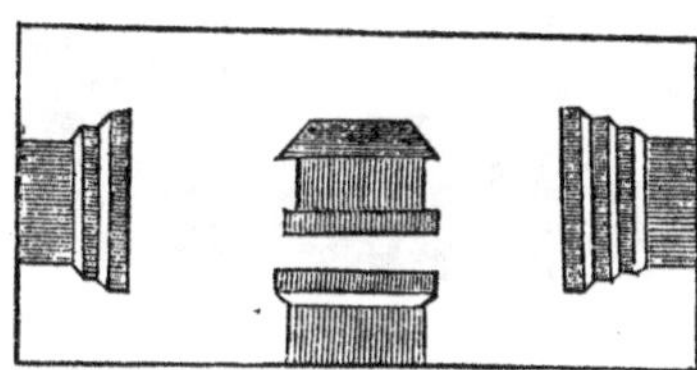

From East to West, and between the North and the South, Freemasonry extends; and in every clime are Masons to be found.

Our institution is said to be supported by *Wisdom*, *Strength*, and *Beauty*, because it is necessary that their should be wisdom to contrive, strength to support, and beauty to adorn all great and important undertakings.

Its *covering* is no less than a clouded canopy—or

starry-decked heaven, where all good Masons hope at last to arrive, by the aid of the theological ladder, which

Jacob, in his vision, saw ascending from earth to heaven; the *three principal rounds* of which are denominated *Faith, Hope,* and *Charity;* and which admonish us to have faith in God, hope in immortality, and charity to all mankind. The greatest of these is *Charity;* for our Faith will be lost in sight, Hope ends in fruition, but Charity extends beyond the grave, through the boundless realms of eternity.

Every well governed Lodge is *furnished* with the *Holy Bible, square,* and *compasses.* The Holy Bible is dedicated to God; the square to the Master; and the compasses to the Craft. The Bible is dedicated to God, because it is the inestimable gift of God to man, * * * * *; the square to the Master, because it is the proper masonic emblem of his office, and should continually remind him of the duty that he owes to the Lodge over which he is elected to preside; and the compasses to the Craft, because by a due attention to their use, they are taught to circumscribe their desires, and keep their passions within due bounds.

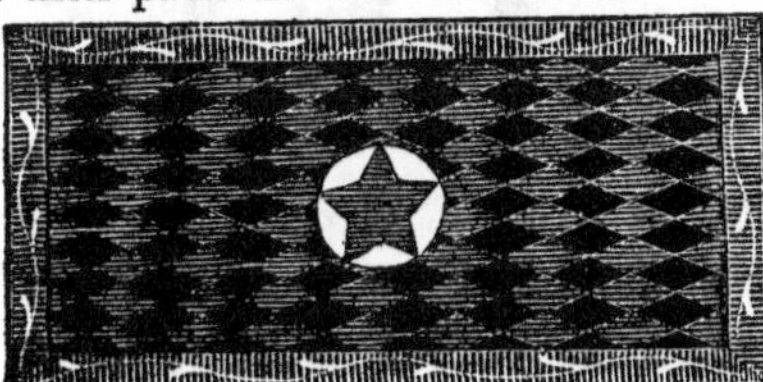

The *ornaments* of a Lodge are, the *mosaic pavement, indented tessel,* and the *blazing star*. The *mosaic pavement* is a representation of the ground-floor of king Solomon's temple; the *indented tessel,* of that beautifully tessellated border or skirting which surrounded it; and the *blazing star* in the center, is commemorative of that star which appeared to guide the wise men of the east to the place of our Saviour's nativity.

The *mosaic pavement* is emblematical of human life, checkered with good and evil; the *beautiful border* which surrounds it, of those manifold blessings and comforts that surround us—and which we hope to enjoy, by a faithful reliance on Divine Providence, which is hieroglyphically represented by the blazing star in the center.

*　　*　　*　　*　　*

The *immoveable* and *moveable jewels* also claim our attention in this section.

* * * * * * *

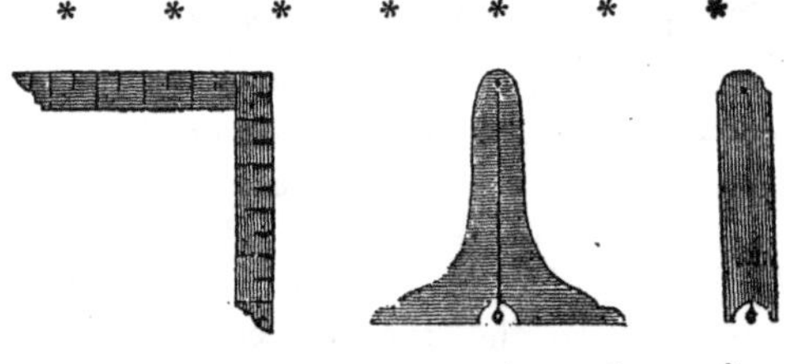

* * * * * * *

The *rough ashler* is a stone as taken from the quarry in its rude and natural state.

The *perfect ashler* is a stone made ready by the hands of the workmen to be adjusted by the working tools of the Fellow-craft.

The *trestle board* is for the master workman to draw his designs upon.

By the rough ashler we are reminded of our rude and imperfect state by nature; by the perfect ashler, of that state of perfection at which we hope to arrive by a virtuous education, our own endeavors, and the blessing of God; and by the trestle board we are also reminded that, as the operative workman erects his temporal building agreeably to the rules and designs laid down by the Master on his trestle board, so should we, both operative and speculative, endeavor to erect our spiritual building agreeably to the rules and designs laid down by the Supreme Architect of the Universe, in the great book of revelation, which is our spiritual, moral, and masonic trestle board.

Lodges were anciently dedicated to king Solomon, as it is said he was the first Most Excellent Grand Master; but Masons professing Christianity dedicate theirs to St. John the Baptist and St. John the Evangelist, who were two eminent Christian patrons of masonry; and since their time, there is, or ought to be represented, in every regular and well-governed Lodge, a certain *point within a circle;* the *point* representing an individual brother; the *circle*, the boundary line of his conduct, beyond which he is never to suffer his preju-

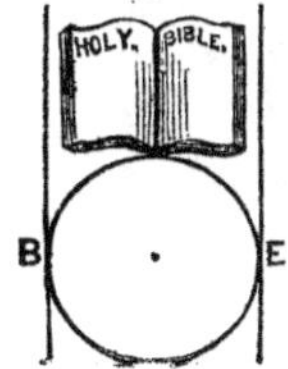

dices or passions to betray him. This *circle* is embordered by two perpendicular parallel *lines*, representing St. John the Baptist and St. John the Evangelist; and upon the top rests the Holy Scriptures. In going round this circle, we necessarily touch upon these two lines, as well as upon the Holy Scriptures; and while a Mason keeps himself circumscribed within their precepts, it is impossible that he should materially err.

* * * * * *

OF BROTHERLY LOVE.

By the exercise of brotherly love, we are taught to regard the whole human species as one family, the high and low, the rich and poor, who, as created by one Almighty Parent, and inhabitants of the same planet, are to aid, support, and protect each other. On this principle, Masonry unites men of every country, sect and opinion, and conciliates true friendship among those who might otherwise have remained at a perpetual distance.

OF RELIEF.

To relieve the distressed, is a duty incumbent on all men; but particularly on Masons, who are linked together by an indissoluble chain of sincere affection. To soothe the unhappy, to sympathise with their misfortunes, to compassionate their miseries, and to restore peace to their troubled minds, is the grand aim we have in view. On this basis we form our friendships and establish our connexions.

OF TRUTH.

Truth is a divine attribute, and the foundation of every virtue. To be good and true, is the first lesson we are taught in masonry. On this theme we contemplate, and by its dictates endeavor to regulate our conduct; hence, while influenced by this principle, hypocrisy and deceit are unknown amongst us, sincerity and plain dealing distinguish us, and the heart and tongue join in promoting each other's welfare, and rejoicing at each other's prosperity.

* * * * *

To this illustration succeeds an explanation of the four cardinal virtues—*temperance*, *fortitude*, *prudence*, and *justice*.

OF TEMPERANCE.

Temperance is that due restraint upon our affections and passions, which renders the body tame and governable, and frees the mind from the allurements of vice. This virtue should be the constant practice of every Mason, as he is thereby taught to avoid excess, or contracting any licentious or vicious habit, the indulgence of which might lead him to disclose some of those valuable secrets which he has promised to conceal and never reveal, and which would consequently subject him to the contempt and detestation of all good Masons. * * * * * *

OF FORTITUDE.

Fortitude is that noble and steady purpose of the mind, whereby we are enabled to undergo any pain, peril, or danger, when prudentially deemed expedient. This virtue is equally distant from rashness and cowardice; and like the former, should be deeply impressed upon the mind of every Mason, as a safe-guard or security against any illegal attack that may be made, by force or otherwise, to extort from him any of those secrets with which he has been so solemnly entrusted; and which virtue was emblematically represented upon his first admission into the Lodge. * * * * * * * * *

OF PRUDENCE.

Prudence teaches us to regulate our lives and actions agreeably to the dictates of reason, and is that habit by which we wisely judge, and prudentially determine, on all things relative to our present, as well as our future happiness. This virtue should be the particular characteristic of every Mason, not only while in the Lodge, but also when abroad in the world; it should be particularly attended to in all strange or mixed companies, never to let fall the least sign, token, or word, whereby the secrets of masonry might be unlawfully obtained. * * * *

OF JUSTICE.

Justice is that standard or boundary of right, which enables us to render to every man his just due without distinction. This virtue is not only consistent with divine and human law, but is the very cement and support of civil society; and, as justice in a great measure constitutes the real good man, so should it be the invariable practice of every Mason never to deviate from the minutest principles thereof. * *

The illustration of these virtues is accompanied with some general observations peculiar to Masons.

Such is the arrangement of the different sections in the first lecture, which, with the forms adopted at the opening and closing of a Lodge, comprehend the whole of the first degree of masonry. The whole is a regular system of morality; conceived in a strain of interesting allegory, which must unfold its beauties to the candid and industrious enquirer.

Charge at Initiation into the First Degree.

Brother—As you are now introduced into the first principles of masonry, I congratulate you on being accepted into this ancient and honorable order; ancient, as having existed from time immemorial; and honorable, as tending in every particular so to render all men who will conform to its precepts. No human institution was ever raised on a better principle, or more solid foundation; nor were ever more excellent rules and useful maxims laid down than are inculcated in the several masonic lectures. The greatest and best of men in all ages have been encouragers and promoters of the art, and have never deemed it derogatory to their dignity to level themselves with the fraternity, extend their privileges, and patronize their assemblies.

There are *three great duties,* which, as a Mason, you are srictly to observe and inculcate—to God, your neighbor, and yourself. To God in never mentioning his name but with that reverential awe which is due from a creature to his Creator; to implore his aid in all your laudable undertakings, and to esteem Him as your chief good. To your neighbor, in acting upon the square, and doing unto him as you would he should do unto you: and to yourself, in avoiding all irregularity and intemperance, which may impair your faculties, or debase the dignity of your profession. A zealous attachment to these duties will insure public and private esteem.

In the State you are to be a quiet and peaceable citizen, true to your government, and just to your country; you are not to countenance disloyalty or rebellion, but patiently submit to legal authority and conform with cheerfulness to the government of the country in which you live.

In your outward demeanor be particularly careful to avoid censure or reproach. Let not interest, favor or prejudice, bias your integrity, or influence you to be guilty of a dishonorable action. And although your frequent appearance at our regular meetings is earnestly solicited, yet it is not meant that masonry should interfere with your necessary avocations, for these are on no account to be neglected: neither are you to suffer your zeal for the institution to lead you into arguments with those who, through ignorance, may ridicule it. But, at your leisure hours, that you may improve in masonic knowledge, you are to converse with well-informed brethren, who will be always as ready to give, as you will be ready to receive instruction.

Finally—keep sacred and inviolable the mysteries of the order, as these are to distinguish you from the rest of the community and mark your consequence among Masons. If, in the circle of your acquaintance, you find a person desirous of being initiated into masonry, be particularly careful not to recommend him, unless you are convinced he will conform to our rules; that the honor, glory, and reputation of the institution may be firmly established, and the world at large convinced of its good effects.

If the candidate be a Clergyman, add the following:

You, brother, are a preacher of that religion, of which the distinguishing characteristics are universal benevolence and unbounded charity. You cannot, therefore, but be fond of the order, and zealous for the interests of Freemasonry, which, in the strongest manner, inculcates the same charity and benevolence, and which, like that religion, encourages every moral and social virtue; which introduces peace and good will among mankind, and is the center of union to those who otherwise might have remained at a perpetual distance. So that whoever is warmed with the spirit of christianity, must esteem, must love Freemasonry. Such is the nature of our institution, that, in all our Lodges, union is cemented by sincere attachment, hypocrisy and deceit are unknown, and pleasure is reciprocally communicated, by the cheerful observance of every obliging office. Virtue, the grand object in view, luminous as the meridian sun, shines refulgent on the mind, enlivens the heart, and converts cool approbation into warm sympathy and cordial affection.

Though every man, who carefully listens to the dictates of reason, may arrive at a clear persuasion of the beauty and necessity of virtue, both public and private, yet it is a full recommendation of a society to have these pursuits continually in view, as the sole objects of their association: and these are the laudable bonds which unite *us* in one indissoluble fraternity.

CHAPTER V.

FELLOW CRAFT'S DEGREE.

Section First.

THE first section of the second degree accurately elucidates the mode of instruction into that particular class; and instructs the diligent craftsman how to proceed in the proper arrangement of the ceremonies used on the occasion. The knowledge of this section is absolutely necessary for all craftsmen; and as it recapitulates the ceremony of initiation, and contains many other important particulars, no officer or member of a Lodge should be unacquainted with it.

The following passage of Scripture is here introduced:

"Thus he showed me; and, behold the Lord stood upon a wall made by a plumb-line, with a plumb-line, in his hand. And the Lord said unto me, Amos, what seest thou? And I said, a plumb-line. Then said the Lord, Behold, I will set a plumb-line in the midst of my people Israel: I will not again pass by them any more." *Amos*, vii. 7, 8.

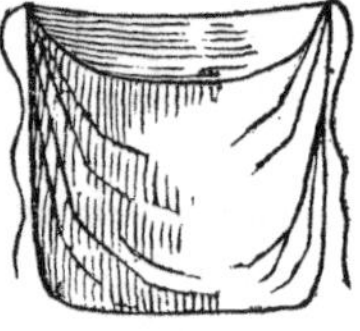

* * * * * * *

The working tools of a fellow craft are here explained —they are the *plumb*, *square*, and *level*.

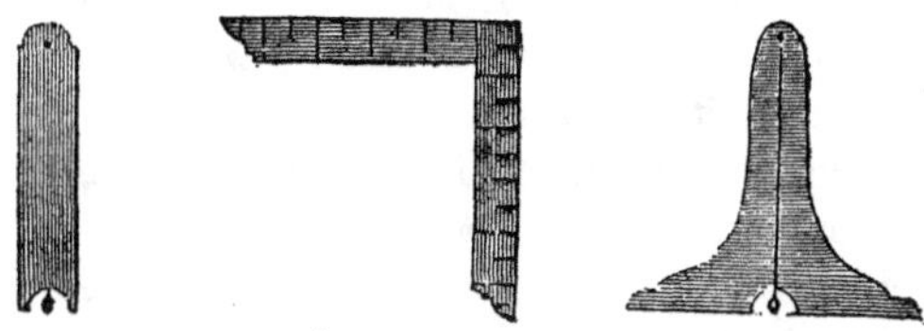

The *plumb* is an instrument made use of by *operative* masons, to raise perpendiculars; the *square*, to square their work; and the *level*, to lay horizontals. But we, as free and accepted Masons, are taught to make use of them for more noble and glorious purposes; the *plumb* admonishes us to walk uprightly in our several stations before God and man; squaring our actions by the *square* of virtue, and remembering that we are travelling upon the *level* of time, to "that undiscovered country, from whose bourne no traveller returns."

Section Second.

The second section of this degree refers to the origin of the institution, and views masonry under two denominations—*operative* and *speculative*.

By *operative* masonry, we allude to a proper application of the useful rules of architecture, whence a structure will derive figure, strength and beauty; and whence will result a due proportion and a just correspondence in all its parts. It furnishes us with dwellings and convenient shelters from the vicissitudes and inclemencies of the seasons; and while it displays the effects of human wisdom, as well in the choice, as in the arrangement, of the sundry materials of which an edifice is composed, it demonstrates that a fund of science and industry is implanted in man for the best, most salutary, and beneficent purposes.

By *speculative* masonry, we learn to subdue the passions, act upon the square, keep a tongue of good report, maintain secrecy and practice charity. It is so far interwoven with religion, as to lay us under obligations to pay that rational homage to the Deity, which at once constitutes our duty and our happiness. It leads the contemplative to view with reverence and admiration the glorious works of creation, and inspires him with the most exalted ideas of the perfections of his divine Creator.

* * * * *

In six days God created the heavens and the earth, and rested on the seventh day; the seventh, therefore, our ancient brethren consecrated as a day of rest from their labors; thereby enjoying frequent opportunities to contemplate the glorious works of creation, and to adore their great Creator.

* * * * *

Peace, Unity, and Plenty are here introduced and explained.

The doctrine of the spheres is included in the science of astronomy, and particularly considered in this section.

The globes are two artificial spherical bodies, on the convex surface of which are represented the countries, seas, and various parts of the earth; the face of the heavens, the planetary revolutions, and other particulars.

The sphere with the parts of the earth delineated on its surface, is called the terrestrial globe; and that with the constellations and other heavenly bodies, the celestial globe.

Their principal use, besides serving as maps to distinguish the outward parts of the earth and the situation of the fixed stars, is to illustrate and explain the phenomena arising from the annual revolution, and the diurnal rotations of the earth round its own axis. They are the noblest instruments for improving the mind, and giving it the most distinct idea of any problem or proposition, as well as enabling it to solve the same. Contemplating these bodies, we are inspired with a due reverence for the Deity and his works, and are induced to encourage the studies of astronomy, geography, navigation, and the arts dependent on them, by which society has been so much benefitted.

The *orders of architecture* come under consideration in this section; a brief description of them may therefore not be improper.

By *order* in architecture, is meant a system of all the members, proportions and ornaments of columns, and pilasters; or, it is the regular arrangement of the projecting parts of a building, which, united with those of a column, form a beautiful, perfect, and complete whole.

From the first formation of society, order in architecture may be traced. When the rigor of the seasons obliged men to contrive shelter from the inclemency of the weather, we learn that they first planted trees on end, and then laid others across to support a covering. The bands which connected those trees at top and bottom, are said to have given rise to the idea of the base and capital of pillars; and from this simple hint originally proceeded the more improved art of architecture.

The five orders are thus classed—the Tuscan, Doric, Ionic, Corinthian, and Composite.

THE TUSCAN

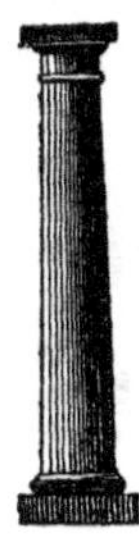

Is the most simple and solid of the five orders. It was invented in Tuscany, whence it derived its name. Its column is seven diameters high; and its capital, base, and entablature have but few mouldings. The simplicity of the construction of this column renders it eligible, where ornament would be superfluous.

THE DORIC,

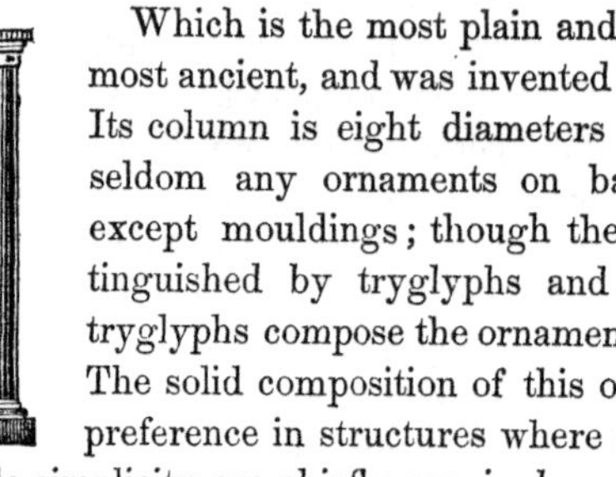

Which is the most plain and natural, is the most ancient, and was invented by the Greeks. Its column is eight diameters high, and has seldom any ornaments on base or capital, except mouldings; though the frieze is distinguished by tryglyphs and metopes, and tryglyphs compose the ornaments of the frieze. The solid composition of this order gives it a preference in structures where strength and a noble simplicity are chiefly required.

The Doric is the best proportioned of all the orders. The several parts of which it is composed are founded on the natural position of solid bodies. In its first invention it was more simple than in its present state. In after-times, when it began to be adorned, it gained the name of Doric; for when it was constructed in its primitive and simple form, the name of Tuscan was conferred on it. Hence the Tuscan precedes the Doric in rank, on account of its resemblance to that pillar in its original state.

THE IONIC

Bears a kind of mean proportion between the more solid and delicate orders. Its column is nine diameters high; its capital is adorned with volutes, and its cornice has dentals. There is both delicacy and ingenuity displayed in this pillar; the invention of which is attributed to the Ionians, as the famous temple of Diana at Ephesus was of this order. It is said to have been formed after the model of an agreeable young woman, of an elegant shape, dressed in her hair, as a contrast to the Doric order, which was formed after that of a strong robust man.

THE CORINTHIAN,

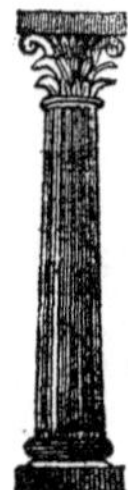

The richest of the five orders, is deemed a master-piece of art. Its column is ten diameters high, and its capital is adorned with two rows of leaves, and eight volutes, which sustain the abacus. The frieze is ornamented with various devices, the cornice with dentals and modillions. This order is used in stately and useful structures.

It was invented at Corinth, by Callimachus, who is said to have taken the hint of the capital of this pillar from the following remarkable circumstance: Accidentally passing by the tomb of a young lady, he perceived a basket of toys covered with a tile, placed over an acanthus root, having been left there by her nurse. As the branches grew up, they encompassed the basket, till, arriving at the tile, they met with an obstruction, and bent downwards. Callimachus struck with the object, set about imitating the figure; the vase of the capital he made to represent the basket; the abacus the tile; and the volutes the bending leaves.

THE COMPOSITE

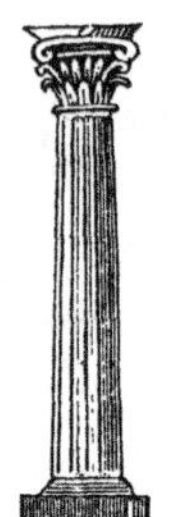

Is compounded of the other orders, and was contrived by the Romans. Its capital has the two rows of leaves of the Corinthian, and the volutes of the Ionic. Its column has the quarter-rounds, as the Tuscan and Doric orders, is ten diameters high, and its cornice has dentals, or simple modillions. This pillar is found in buildings where strength, elegance and beauty are displayed.

The ancient and original orders of architecture, revered by Masons, are no more than three—the Doric, Ionic, and Corinthian, which were invented by the Greeks. To these the Romans have added two—the Tuscan, which they made plainer than the Doric; and the Composite, which was more ornamental, if not more beautiful, than the Corinthian. The first three orders alone, however, show invention and particular character, and essentially differ from each other; the two others have nothing but what is borrowed, and differ only accidentally. The Tuscan is the Doric in its earliest state; and the Composite is the Corinthian enriched with the Ionic. To the Greeks, therefore, and not to the Romans, we are indebted for what is great, judicious, and distinct in architecture.

OF THE FIVE SENSES OF HUMAN NATURE.

An analysis of the human faculties is next given in

this section, in which the five external senses particularly claim attention; these are—hearing, seeing, feeling, smelling and tasting.

HEARING

Is that sense by which we distinguish sounds, and are capable of enjoying all the agreeable charms of music. By it we are enabled to enjoy the pleasures of society, and reciprocally to communicate to each other our thoughts and intentions, our purposes and desires; while thus our reason is capable of exerting its utmost power and energy.

The wise and beneficent Author of Nature intended, by the formation of this sense, that we should be social creatures, and receive the greatest and most important part of our knowledge by the information of others. For these purposes we are endowed with hearing, that, by a proper exertion of our natural powers, our happiness may be complete.

SEEING

Is that sense by which we distinguish objects, and in an instant of time, without change of place or situation, view armies in battle array, figures of the most stately structures, and all the agreeable variety displayed in the landscape of nature. By this we find our way in the pathless ocean, traverse the globe of earth, determine its figure and dimensions, and delineate any region or quarter of it. By it we measure the planetary orbs, and make new discoveries in the sphere of the fixed stars. Nay, more—by it we perceive the tempers and dispositions, the passions and affections, of our fellow creatures, when they wish most to conceal them; so that, though the tongue may be taught to lie and dissemble, the countenance would display the hypocrisy to the discerning eye. In fine, the rays of light which administer to this sense, are the most astonishing parts of animated creation, and render the eye a peculiar object of admiration.

Of all the faculties, sight is the noblest. The structure of the eye and its appurtenances, evince the admirable contrivance of nature for performing all its various external and internal motions; while the variety displayed in the eyes of different animals, suited to their several ways of life, clearly demonstrates this organ to be the master-piece of nature's work.

FEELING

Is that sense by which we distinguish the different qualities of bodies—such as heat and cold, hardness and softness, roughness and smoothness, figure, solidity, motion, and extension.

These three senses—*hearing, seeing, and feeling*—are deemed peculiarly essential among Masons.

SMELLING

Is that sense by which we distinguish odors, the various kinds of which convey different impressions to the mind. Animal and vegetable bodies, and indeed most other bodies, while exposed to the air, continually send forth effluvia of vast subtlety, as well in a state of life and growth, as in a state of fermentation and putrefaction. These effluvia, being drawn into the nostrils along with the air, are the means by which all bodies are smelled. Hence it is evident that there is a manifest appearance of design in the great Creator's having planted the organ of smell in the inside of that canal, through which the air continually passes in respiration.

TASTING

Enables us to make a proper distinction in the choice of our food. The organ of this sense guards the entrance of the alimentary canal, as that of smelling guards the entrance of the canal for respiration. From the situation of both these organs, it is plain that they were intended by nature to distinguish wholesome food from that which is nauseous. Every thing that enters into the stomach must undergo the scrutiny of tasting; and by it we are capable of discerning the changes which the same body undergoes in the different compositions of art, cookery, chemistry, pharmacy, &c.

Smelling and tasting are inseparably connected, and it is by the unnatural kind of life men commonly lead in society, that these senses are rendered less fit to perform their natural offices.

On the mind all our knowledge must depend; what,

therefore, can be a more proper subject for the investigation of Masons? By anatomical dissection and observation, we become acquainted with the body; but it is by the anatomy of the mind alone we discover its powers and principles.

To sum up the whole of this transcendent measure of God's bounty to man, we shall add, that *memory, imagination, taste, reasoning, moral perception,* and all the active powers of the soul, present a vast and boundless field for philosophical disquisition, which far exceeds human inquiry, and are peculiar mysteries, known only to nature and nature's God, to whom we are all indebted for creation, preservation, and every blessing we enjoy.

OF THE SEVEN LIBERAL ARTS AND SCIENCES.

The seven liberal arts and sciences are illustrated in this section, which are—*Grammar, Rhetoric, Logic, Arithmetic, Geometry, Music,* and *Astronomy.*

GRAMMAR.

Grammar teaches the proper arrangement of words, according to the idiom or dialect of any particular people; and that excellency of pronunciation, which enables us to speak or write a language with accuracy, agreeably to reason and correct usage.

RHETORIC.

Rhetoric teaches us to speak copiously and fluently on any subject, not merely with propriety alone, but with all the advantage of force and elegance; wisely contriving to captivate the hearer by strength of argument and beauty of expression, whether it be to entreat and exhort, to admonish or approve.

LOGIC.

Logic teaches us to guide our reason discretionally in the general knowledge of things, and directs our inquiries after truth. It consists of a regular train of argument, whence we infer, deduce, and conclude, according to certain premises laid down, admitted, or granted; and in it are employed the faculties of conceiving, judging, reasoning, and disposing; all of which are naturally led on from one gradation to another, till the point in question is finally determined.

ARITHMETIC.

Arithmetic teaches the powers and properties of numbers, which is variously effected—by letters, tables, figures and instruments. By this art, reasons and demonstrations are given for finding out any certain numbers, whose relation or affinity to another is already known or discovered.

GEOMETRY.

Geometry treats of the powers and properties of magnitudes in general, where length, breadth and thickness are considered, from a *point* to a *line*, from a line to a *superfices*, and from a superfices to a *solid*.

A point is a dimensionless figure; or an indivisible part of space.

A line is a point continued, and a figure of one capacity, namely, length.

A superfices is a figure of two dimensions, namely, length and breadth.

A solid is a figure of three dimensions, namely, length, breadth and thickness.

By this science the architect is enabled to conduct his plans, and execute his designs—the general to arrange his soldiers—the engineer to mark out ground for encampments—the geographer to give us the dimensions of the world, and all things therein contained; to delineate the extent of seas, and specify the divisions of empires, kingdoms and provinces—by it, also, the astronomer is enabled to make his observations, and to fix the duration of seasons, years and cycles. In fine, geometry is the foundation of architecture and the root of the mathematics.

MUSIC.

Music teaches the art of forming concords, so as to compose delightful harmony, by a mathematical and proportional arrangement of acute, grave and mixed sounds. This art, by a series of experiments, is reduced to a demonstration, with respect to tones and the intervals of sounds; inquires into the nature of concords and discords, and enables us to find out the proportion between them by numbers.

ASTRONOMY.

Astronomy is that divine art by which we are taught to read the wisdom, strength, and beauty of the Almighty Creator, in those sacred pages, the celestial hemisphere. Assisted by astronomy, we can observe the motions, measure the distances, comprehend the magnitudes, and calculate the periods and eclipses of the heavenly bodies. By it we learn the use of the globes, the system of the world, and the preliminary law of nature. While we are employed in the study of this science, we must perceive unparalleled instances of wisdom and goodness, and, through the whole creation, trace the glorious Author by his works.

Here an emblem of plenty is introduced and explained.

CORN. WINE. OIL.

* * * * *

OF THE MORAL ADVANTAGES OF GEOMETRY.

Geometry, the first and noblest of sciences, is the basis upon which the superstructure of masonry is erected. By geometry we may curiously trace nature, through her various windings, to her most concealed recesses. By it we discover the power, the wisdom, and the goodness of the Grand Artificer of the Universe, and view with delight the proportions which connect this vast machine. By it we discover how the planets move in their different orbits, and demonstrate their various revolutions. By it we account for the return of the seasons, and the variety of scenes which each season displays to the discerning eye. Numerous worlds are around us, all formed by the same Divine Artist, and which roll through the vast expanse, and are all conducted by the same unerring law of nature.

A survey of nature, and the observation of her

beautiful proportions, first determined man to imitate the divine plan, and study symmetry and order. This gave rise to societies, and birth to every useful art. The architect began to design, and the plans which he laid down, being improved by experience and time, have produced works which are the admiration of every age.

The lapse of time, the ruthless hand of ignorance, and the devastations of war, have laid waste and destroyed many valuable monuments of antiquity, on which the utmost exertions of human genius have been employed. Even the Temple of Solomon, so spacious and magnificent, and constructed by so many celebrated artists, escaped not the unsparing ravages of barbarous force. Freemasonry, notwithstanding, has still survived. The *attentive ear* receives the sound from the *instructive tongue*, and the mysteries of masonry are safely lodged in the repository of faithful breasts. Tools and implements of architecture are selected by the fraternity, to imprint on the memory wise and serious truths; and thus, through a succession of ages, are transmitted unimpaired the excellent tenets of our institution. * * * * * *

CHARGE.

Brother—Being passed to the second degree of masonry, we congratulate you on your preferment. The internal, and not the external qualifications of a man, are what masonry regards. As you increase in knowledge you will improve in social intercourse.

It is unnecessary to recapitulate the duties which, as a Mason, you are bound to discharge, or to enlarge on the necessity of a strict adherence to them, as your own experience must have established their value.

Our laws and regulations you are strenuously to support, and be always ready to assist in seeing them duly executed. You are not to palliate, or aggravate, the offences of your brethren; but in the decision of every trespass against our rules, you are to judge with candor, admonish with friendship, and reprehend with justice.

The study of the liberal arts, that valuable branch of education, which tends so effectually to polish and adorn the mind, is earnestly recommended to your consideration—especially the science of geometry, which is established as the basis of our art. Geometry, or masonry, originally synonymous terms, being of a divine and moral nature, is enriched with the most useful knowledge; while it proves the wonderful properties of nature, it demonstrates the more important truths of morality.

Your past behaviour and regular deportment have merited the honor which we have now conferred; and in your new character it is expected that you will conform to the principles of the Order, by steadily persevering in the practice of every commendable virtue.

Such is the nature of your engagements as a fellow-craft; and to these duties you are bound by the most sacred ties.

CHAPTER VI.

MASTER MASON'S DEGREE.

GENERAL REMARKS.

From this class the rulers of regular bodies of Masons, in the first three degrees, are selected; as it is only from those who are capable of giving instruction, that we can expect to receive it.

The ceremonies attending this stage of our profession are solemn; during which a sacred awe is diffused over the mind.

The following passage of Scripture is introduced during the ceremonies:

"Remember now thy Creator in the days of thy youth, while the evil days come not, nor the years draw nigh, when thou shalt say, I have no pleasure in them; while the sun, or the light, or the moon, or the stars be not darkened, nor the clouds return after the rain: In the day when the keepers of the house shall tremble, and the strong men shall bow themselves, and the grinders cease because they are few, and those that look out of the windows be darkened, and the doors shall be shut in the streets, when the sound of the grinding is low, and he shall rise up at the voice of the bird, and all the daughters of music shall be brought low; also when they shall be afraid of that which is high, and fears shall be in the way, and the almond tree shall flourish, and the grasshopper shall be a burden, and desire shall fail; because man goeth to his long home, and the mourners go about the streets: Or ever the silver cord be loosed, or the golden bowl be broken, or the pitcher be broken at the fountain, or the wheel broken at the cistern. Then shall the dust return to the earth as it was; and the spirit shall return unto God who gave it." *Ecclesiastes*, xii. 1–7.

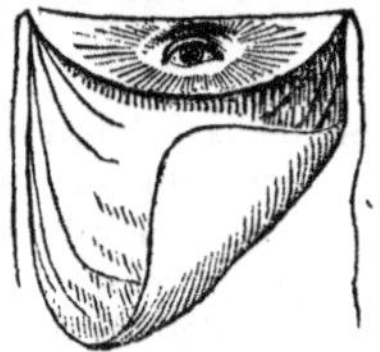

The *working tools* of a Master Mason are all the implements of masonry appertaining to the first three degrees indiscriminately, but more especially the *trowel.*

The TROWEL is an instrument made use of by operative masons to spread the cement which unites a building into one common mass; but we, as free and accepted Masons, are taught to make use of it for the more noble and glorious purpose of spreading the cement of *brotherly love* and affection; that cement which unites us into one sacred band, or society of friends and brothers, among whom no contention should ever exist, but that noble contention, or rather emulation, of who can best work and best agree.

Section Second.

This section recites the historical traditions of the order, and presents to view a finished picture of the utmost consequence to the fraternity. It exemplifies an instance of virtue, fortitude, and integrity, seldom equalled, and never excelled, in the history of man.

* * * * * * *

FUNERAL DIRGE.

PLEYEL.

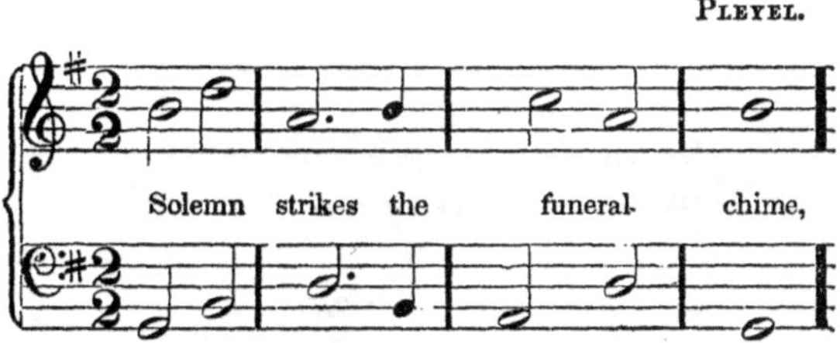

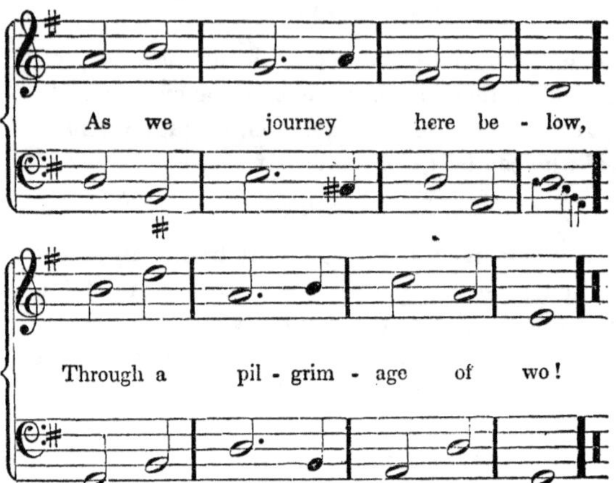

Mortals, now indulge a tear,
For mortality is near!
See how wide her trophies wave
O'er the slumbers of the grave!

Here another guest we bring,
Seraphs of celestial wing,
To our funeral altar come,
Waft this Friend and Brother home.

Lord of all! below—above—
Fill our hearts with Truth and Love;
When dissolves our earthly tie,
Take us to thy Lodge on high.

PRAYER.

Thou, O God! knowest our down-sitting and our up-rising, and understandest our thoughts afar off. Shield and defend us from the evil intentions of our enemies, and support us under the trials and afflictions we are destined to endure, while travelling through this vale of tears. Man that is born of a woman, is of few days and full of trouble. He cometh forth as a flower, and is cut down; he fleeth also as a shadow, and continueth not. Seeing his days are determined, the number of his months are with thee; thou hast appointed his bounds that he cannot pass; turn from him that he may rest, till he shall accomplish his day. For there is hope of a tree, if it be cut down, that it will sprout again, and that the tender branch thereof will not cease. But man dieth and wasteth away; yea, man giveth up the ghost, and where is he? As the waters fail from the sea, and the flood decayeth and drieth up, so man lieth down, and riseth not up till the heavens shall be no more. Yet, O Lord! have compassion on the children of thy creation, administer them comfort in time of trouble, and save them with an everlasting salvation. Amen.

Response—*So mote it be.*

Section Third.

In this branch of the lecture, many particulars relative to King Solomon's Temple are considered.

The construction of this grand edifice was attended with two remarkable circumstances. From Josephus we learn, that although seven years were occupied in building it, yet during the whole term it rained not in the day time, that the workmen might not be obstructed in their labor; and from sacred history it appears that there was neither the sound of the hammer, nor axe, nor any tool of iron, heard in the house while it was building.

This famous fabric was supported by fourteen hundred and fifty-three columns, and two thousand nine hundred and six pilasters—all hewn from the finest Parian marble. There were employed in its building three Grand Masters; three thousand and three hundred Masters, or overseers of the work; eighty thousand Fellow Crafts, or hewers on the mountains and in the quarries; and seventy thousand Entered Apprentices, or bearers of burdens. All these were classed and arranged in such a manner, by the wisdom of Solomon, that neither envy, discord, nor confusion were suffered to interrupt that universal peace and tranquility, which pervaded the world at that important period.

7 { 1 — 6

5 { 2 — 3

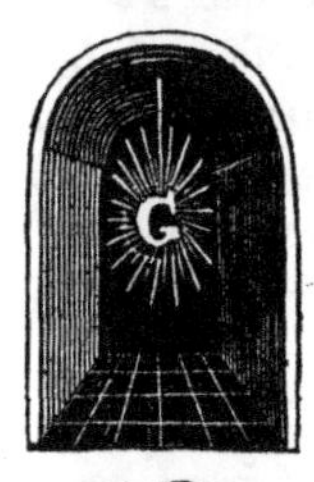

3

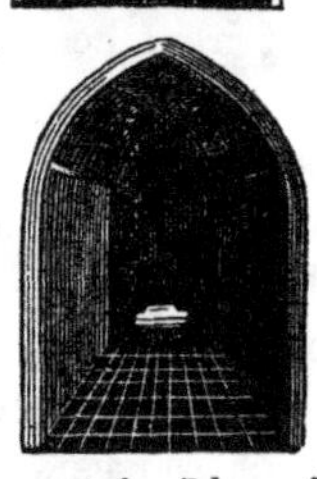

This section also illustrates certain hieroglyphical emblems, and inculcates many useful lessons, to extend knowledge and promote virtue.

THE THREE STEPS

Usually delineated upon the Master's carpet, are emblematical of the three principal stages of human life, viz.—youth, manhood, and age. In youth, as entered apprentices, we ought industriously to occupy our minds in the attainment of useful knowledge; in manhood, as fellow crafts, we should apply our knowledge to the discharge of our respective duties to God, our neighbors, and ourselves; so that in age, as master masons, we may enjoy the happy reflections consequent on a well-spent life, and die in the hope of a glorious immortality.

THE POT OF INCENSE

Is an emblem of a pure heart, which is always an acceptable sacrifice to the Deity; and as this glows with fervent heat, so should our hearts continually glow with gratitude to the great and beneficent Author of our existence, for the manifold blessings and comforts we enjoy.

THE BEE HIVE

Is an emblem of industry, and recommends the practice of that virtue to all created beings, from the highest seraph in heaven, to the lowest reptile of the dust. It teaches us, that as we come into the world rational and intelligent beings, so we should ever be industrious ones; never sitting down contented while our fellow creatures around us are in want, when it is in our power to relieve them without inconvenience to ourselves.

When we take a survey of nature, we view man in his infancy, more helpless and indigent than the brute creation; he lies languishing for days, months, and years totally incapable of providing sustenance for himself, of guarding against the attack of the wild beasts of the forest, or sheltering himself from the inclemencies of the weather.

It might have pleased the great Creator of heaven and earth to have made man independent of all other beings; but, as dependence is one of the strongest bonds of society, mankind were made dependent on each other for protection and security, as they thereby enjoy better opportunities of fulfilling the duties of reciprocal love and friendship. Thus was man formed for social and active life, the noblest part of the work of God; and he that will so demean himself as not to be endeavoring to add to the common stock of knowledge and understanding, may be deemed a *drone* in the *hive* of nature, a useless member of society, and unworthy of our protection as Masons.

THE BOOK OF CONSTITUTIONS, GUARDED BY THE TYLER'S SWORD,

Reminds us that we should be ever watchful and guarded in our thoughts, words and actions, particularly when before the enemies of masonry; ever bearing in remembrance those truly masonic virtues, *silence* and *circumspection*.

THE SWORD POINTING TO A NAKED HEART,

Demonstrates that justice will sooner or later overtake us; and although our thoughts, words and actions may be hidden from the eyes of man, yet that

ALL-SEEING EYE!

Whom the *Sun, Moon,* and *Stars* obey, and under whose watchful care even comets perform their stupendous revolutions, beholds the inmost recesses of the human heart, and will reward us according to our works.

THE ANCHOR AND ARK

Are emblems of a well-grounded *hope,* and a well-spent life. They are emblematical of that divine *ark* which safely bears us over this tempestuous sea of troubles, and that *anchor* which shall safely moor us in a peaceful harbor, where the wicked cease from troubling, and the weary shall find rest.

THE FORTY-SEVENTH PROBLEM OF EUCLID.*

This was an invention of our ancient friend and brother, the great Pythagoras, who, in his travels through Asia, Africa, and Europe, was raised to the sublime degree of Master Mason, and initiated into several orders of priesthood. This wise philosopher enriched his mind abundantly in a general knowledge of things, and more especially in geometry or masonry. On this subject he drew out many problems and theorems, and amongst the most distinguished, he erected this, which in the joy of his heart he called *Eureka*, in the Grecian language, signifying *I have found it;* and upon the discovery of which, he is said to have sacrificed a hecatomb. It teaches Masons to be general lovers of the arts and sciences.

THE HOUR-GLASS

Is an emblem of human life. Behold! how swiftly the sands run, and how rapidly our lives are drawing to a close. We cannot without astonishment behold the little particles which are contained in this machine, how they pass away almost imperceptibly, and yet, to our surprise, in the short space of an hour they are all exhausted.

---

*THEOREM—In any right-angled triangle, the square which is described upon the side subtending the right angle, is equal to the squares described upon the sides which contain the right angle.

Thus wastes man! To-day he puts forth the tender leaves of hope; to-morrow, blossoms, and bears his blushing honors thick upon him; the next day comes a frost, which nips the shoot, and when he thinks his greatness still aspiring, he falls, like autumn leaves, to enrich our mother earth.

THE SCYTHE

Is an emblem of time, which cuts the brittle thread of life, and launches us into eternity. Behold! what havoc the scythe of time makes among the human race; if by chance we should escape the numerous evils incident to childhood and youth, and with health and vigor arrive at the years of manhood, yet withal we must soon be cut down by the all-devouring scythe of time, and be gathered into the land where our fathers have gone before us.

* * * * *

Then let us imitate the Christian in his virtuous and amiable conduct. In his unfeigned piety to God. In his inflexible fidelity to his trust: that we may welcome the grim tyrant Death, and receive him as a kind messenger sent to translate us from this imperfect, to that all perfect, glorious, and celestial Lodge above, where the Supreme Architect of the universe presides.

CHARGE.

BROTHER—Your zeal for the institution of masonry, the progress you have made in the mystery, and your conformity to our regulations, have pointed you out as a proper object for our favor and esteem.

You are now bound by duty, honor and gratitude, to be faithful to your trust; to support the dignity of your character on every occasion; and to enforce, by precept and example, obedience to the tenets of the order.

In the character of a Master Mason, you are authorized to correct the errors and irregularities of your uninformed brethren, and to guard them against a breach of fidelity. To preserve the reputation of the fraternity unsullied, must be your constant care; and for this purpose it is your province to recommend to your inferiors, obedience and submission; to your equals, courtesy and affability; to your superiors, kindness and condescension. Universal benevolence you are always to cultivate; and by the regularity of your own behaviour, afford the best example for the conduct of others less informed. The ancient landmarks of the order, entrusted to your care, you are carefully to preserve; and never suffer them to be infringed, or countenance a deviation from the established usages and customs of the fraternity.

Your virtue, honor, and reputation are concerned in supporting with dignity the character you now bear. Let no motive, therefore, make you swerve from your duty, violate your vows, or betray your trust; but be true and faithful, and imitate the example of that celebrated artist whom you this evening represent. Thus you will render yourself deserving of the honor which we have conferred, and merit the confidence we have reposed.

PART SECOND.

CHAPTER I.

MARK MASTER'S DEGREE.

This degree of masonry was not less useful in its original institution, nor are its effects less beneficial to mankind, than those which precede it.

By the influence of this degree, each operative mason at the erection of King Solomon's temple, was known and distinguished by the Senior Grand Warden. If defects were found, the overseers were enabled, without difficulty, to ascertain who was the faulty workman: so that deficiencies might be remedied, without injuring the credit or diminishing the reward of the industrious and faithful of the craft.

CHARGE TO BE READ AT OPENING.

"Wherefore, brethern, lay aside all malice, and guile, and hypocricies, and envies, and all evil speakings. If so be ye have tasted that the Lord is gracious; to whom coming, as unto a living stone, disallowed indeed of men, but chosen of God, and precious; ye, also, as living stones, be ye built up a spiritual house, an holy priesthood, to offer up sacrifices acceptable to God.

Wherefore, also, it is contained in the Scriptures, Behold, I lay in Zion, for a foundation, a tried stone, a precious corner stone, a sure foundation; he that believeth, shall not make haste to pass it over. Unto you, therefore, which believe, it is an honor; and even to them which be disobedient, the stone which the builders disallowed, the same is made the head of the corner.

Brethren, this is the will of God, that with well-doing ye put to silence the ignorance of foolish men. As free, and not using your liberty for a cloak of maliciousness, but as the servants of God. Honor all men, love the brotherhood; fear God."

Section First.

The first section contains the manner of opening a Mark Master's Lodge. It teaches the stations and duties of the respective officers, and recapitulates the mystic ceremonies of introducing a candidate.

In this section is exemplified the regularity and good order that was observed by the craftsmen on Mount Libanus. and in the plains and quarries of Zeredatha, and it ends with a beautiful display of the manner in which one of the principal events originated, which characterizes this degree.

Section Second.

In the second section the Mark Master is particularly instructed in the origin and history of this degree, and the indispensable obligations he is under to stretch forth his assisting hand to the relief of an indigent and worthy brother, to a certain and specified extent.

In the course of the lecture, the following texts of Scripture are introduced and explained:

"Then he brought me back the way of the gate of the outward sanctuary which looketh toward the east; and it was shut. Then said the Lord unto me: This gate shall be shut, it shall not be opened, and no man shall enter in by it; because the Lord the God of Israel, hath entered in by it; therefore it shall be shut. It is for the prince; the prince he shall sit in it to eat bread before the Lord; he shall enter by the way of the porch of that gate, and shall go out by the way of the same. And the Lord said unto me, Son of man, mark well, and behold with thine eyes, and hear with thine ears all that I say unto thee concerning all the ordinances of the house of the Lord, and all the laws thereof; and mark well the entering in of the house, with every going forth of the Sanctuary." *Ezekiel*, xliv. 1–3–5.

The stone which the builders refused is become the head stone of the corner. *Psalms*, cxviii. 22.

Did ye never read in the Scriptures, the stone which the builders rejected, the same is become the head of the corner? *Matt.* xxi. 42.

And have ye not read in the Scripture; the stone which the builders rejected, is become the head of the corner? *Mark*, vii. 10.

This is the stone which was set at naught of you builders, which is become the head of the corner. *Acts*, iv. 11.

To him that overcometh will I give to eat of the hidden manna, and will give him a *white stone*, and in the stone a *new name* written, which no man knoweth saving him that receiveth it. *Rev.* ii. 17."

The *working tools* of a Mark Master are the *chisel* and *mallet*.

The *chisel* morally demonstrates the advantages of discipline and education. The mind, like the diamond in its original state, is rude and unpolished; but as the effect of the chisel on the external coat soon presents to view the latent beauties of the diamond, so education discovers the latent virtues of the mind, and draws them forth to range the large field of matter and space, to display the summit of human knowledge, our duty to God and to man.

The *mallet* morally teaches to correct irregularities, and to reduce man to a proper level; so that by quiet deportment he may, in the school of discipline, learn to be content. What the mallet is to the workman, enlightened reason is to the passions; it curbs ambition, it represses envy, it moderates anger, and it encourages good dispositions; whence arises, among good Masons, that comely order,

"Which nothing earthly gives, or can destroy—
The soul's calm sunshine and the heartfelt joy."

CHARGE.

Brother—I congratulate you on being thought worthy of being promoted to this honorable degree of masonry. Permit me to impress it on your mind, that your assiduity should ever be commensurate with your duties, which become more and more extensive as you advance in masonry.

The situation to which you are now promoted will

draw upon you not only the scrutinizing eyes of the world at large, but those also of your brethren, on whom this degree of masonry has not been conferred: all will be justified in expecting your conduct and behaviour to be such as may with safety be imitated.

In the honorable character of Mark Master Mason, it is more particularly your duty to endeavor to let your conduct in the world, as well as in the Lodge and among your brethren, be such as may stand the test of the Grand Overseer's square; that you may not, like the unfinished and imperfect work of the negligent and unfaithful of former times, be rejected and thrown aside, as unfit for that spiritual building, that house not made with hands, eternal in the heavens.

While such is your conduct, should misfortunes assail you, should friends forsake you, should envy traduce your good name, and malice persecute you; yet you may have confidence that, among Mark Master Masons, you will find friends who will administer relief to your distresses, and comfort your afflictions; ever bearing in mind, as a consolation under all the frowns of fortune, and as an encouragement to hope for better prospects, that *the stone which the builders rejected*, possessing merits to them unknown, *became the chief stone of the corner*.

MARK MASTER'S SONG.

You who have pass'd the square,
For your rewards prepare,
Join heart and hand;
Each with his mark in view,
March with the just and true;
Wages to you are due
At your command.

Hiram, the widow's son,
Sent unto Solomon
Our great key-stone;
On it appears the name
Which raises high the fame
Of all to whom the same
Is truly known.

Now to the westward move,
Where, full of strength and love,
Hiram doth stand;
But if impostors are
Mix'd with the worthy there,
Caution them to beware
Of the right hand.

Now to the praise of those
Who triumph'd o'er the foes
Of mason's art;
To the praiseworthy three,
Who founded this degree;
May all their virtues be
Deep in our hearts.

Previous to closing the Lodge, the following parable is recited:

"For the kingdom of heaven is like unto a man that is a householder, which went out early in the morning to hire laborers into his vineyard. And when he had agreed with the laborers for a penny a day, he sent them into his vineyard. And he went out about the third hour, and saw others standing idle in the market place, and said unto them, go ye also into the vineyard, and whatsoever is right I will give you. And they went their way. Again he went out about the sixth and ninth hour, and did likewise. And about the eleventh hour he went out and found others standing idle, and saith unto them, why stand ye here all the day idle? They say unto him, because no man hath hired us. He saith unto them, go ye also into the vineyard, and whatsoever is right, that shall ye receive. So, when even was come, the lord of the vineyard saith unto his steward, call the laborers, and give them their hire, beginning from the last unto the first. And when they came that were hired about the eleventh hour, they received every man a penny: but when the first came, they supposed that they should have received more; and they likewise received every man a penny. And when they had received it, they murmured against the good man of the house, saying, these last have wrought but one hour, and thou hast made them equal unto us, which have borne the burden and heat of the day. But he answered one of them, and said, friend, I do thee no wrong: didst not thou agree with me for a penny? Take that thine is, and go thy way: I will give unto this last, even as unto thee. Is it not lawful for me to do what I will with mine own? Is thine eye evil, because I am good? So the last shall be first, and the first last: for many be called, but few chosen."

Matt. xx. 1–16.

CHAPTER II

PRESENT OR PAST MASTER'S DEGREE.

GENERAL REMARKS.

This degree should be carefully studied and well understood, by every Master of a Lodge. It treats of the government of our society, the disposition of our rulers, and illustrates their requisite qualifications. It includes the ceremony of opening and closing Lodges in the several preceding degrees; and also the forms of installation and consecration. It comprehends the ceremonies at laying the foundation stones of public buildings, and also at dedications and at funerals, by a variety of particulars explanatory of those ceremonies.

Section First.

This section contains the form of a petition for letters of dispensation, or a warrant of constitution for a Lodge, empowering them to work. The ceremonies of constitution and consecration are considered, with the form of a Grand Procession.

FORM OF A PETITION FOR A CHARTER OR WARRANT TO ESTABLISH A NEW LODGE.

To the Most Worshipful Grand Lodge of the State of ———

Your petitioners respectfully represent, that they are *ancient, free, and accepted Master Masons.* Having the prosperity of the Fraternity at heart, they are willing to exert their best endeavors to promote and diffuse the genuine principles of masonry. For the convenience of their respective dwellings, and for other good reasons, they are desirous of forming a new Lodge in the town of ————, to be named ———— Lodge. In consequence of this desire, and for the good of the craft, they pray for a warrant or dispensation, to empower them to assemble as a legal Lodge, to discharge the duties of masonry in the several degrees of Entered Apprentice, Fellow Craft, and Master Mason, in a regular and constitutional manner, according to the ancient form of the fraternity, and the laws and regulations of the Grand Lodge. That they have nominated and do recommend A. B. to be the first Master; C. D. to be the first Senior Warden, and E. F. to be the first Junior Warden of said Lodge; that, if the prayer of the petition should be granted, they promise a strict conformity to all the constitutional laws, rules and regulations of the Grand Lodge.

This petition must be signed by at least eight regular Master Masons, one of whom must be of the degree of Past Master; and recommended by the Lodge nearest the place where the new Lodge is to be held. It must be delivered to the Grand Secretary, whose duty it is to lay it before the Grand Lodge. In the recess of the Grand Lodge, application should be made in the same form to the Grand Master, or the Deputy Grand Master.

After a charter is granted by the Grand Lodge, the Grand Master appoints a day and hour for constituting and consecrating the new Lodge, and for installing the Master, Wardens, and other officers. The Grand

Master has power to appoint some worthy *Past Master*, with full power to consecrate, constitute, and install the petitioners.

CEREMONY OF CONSTITUTION AND CONSECRATION.

On the day and hour appointed, the Grand Master and his officers meet in a convenient room, near the Lodge to be constituted, and open in the third degree. After the officers of the new Lodge are examined by the Deputy Grand Master, they send a messenger to the Grand Master, with the following message, viz:

MOST WORSHIPFUL:—The officers and brethren of ———— Lodge, who are now assembled in their lodge room at ————, have instructed me to inform you, that the Most Worshipful Grand Lodge was pleased to grant them a charter, authorizing them to form and open a Lodge of free and accepted Masons in the town of ————. They are now desirous that their Lodge should be consecrated, and their officers installed in *due and ancient form;* for which purpose they are now met, and await the pleasure of the Most Worshipful Grand Master.

When notice is given, the Grand Lodge walk in procession to the hall of the new Lodge. When the Grand Master enters, the grand honors are given by the new Lodge; the officers of which resign their seats to the grand officers, and take their several stations on the left.

The necessary cautions are given, and all excepting *Present or Past Masters* of Lodges, are requested to retire, until the Master of the new Lodge is inducted into the *Oriental Chair of Solomon.* He is then bound to the faithful performance of his trust, and invested with the characteristics of the chair.

Upon due notice, the Grand Marshal re-conducts the brethren into the hall; and all take their places, except the members of the new Lodge, who form a procession on one side of the hall. As they advance, the Grand Master addresses them :

"Brethren, behold your Master."

They make the proper salutations as they pass.

A grand procession is then formed, in the following order, viz:

Tyler with a drawn sword;
Two Stewards with white rods;
Entered Apprentices;
Fellow Crafts;
Master Masons;
Marshals;
Stewards;
Junior Deacons;
Senior Deacons;
Secretaries;
Treasurers;
Past Wardens;
Junior Wardens;
Senior Wardens;
Past Masters;

Mark Masters;
Royal Arch Masons,
Select Masters;
Knights Templars;
Masters of Lodges;

THE NEW LODGE.

Tyler with a drawn sword;
Stewards with white rods;
Entered Apprentices;
Fellow Crafts;
Master Masons;
Junior and Senior Deacons;
Secretary and Treasurer;
Two brethren carrying the flooring,* or Lodge;
Junior and Senior Wardens;
The Holy Writings, carried by the oldest or some suitable member not in office;
The W. Master;
Music.

THE GRAND LODGE.

Grand Tyler with drawn sword;
Grand Stewards with white rods;
A brother carrying a golden vessel of corn;†
Two brethren carrying the silver vessels, one of wine, the other of oil;
Grand Secretaries;
Grand Treasurer;
A burning Taper, borne by a Past Master;

* Carpet. † Wheat.

A Past Master, bearing the Holy Writings, Square and Compasses, supported by two Stewards with white rods;
Two burning Tapers, borne by two Past Masters;
The Tuscan and Composite Orders;
The Doric, Ionic, and Corinthian Orders;
Past Grand Wardens;
Marshal; Past Deputy Grand Masters;
Past Grand Masters;
The Globes;
Clergy and Orator;
R. W. Junior and Senior Grand Wardens;
R. W. Deputy Grand Master;
The Master of the oldest Lodge, carrying the Book of Constitutions;
The M. W. Grand Master;
The Grand Deacons, on a line seven feet apart, on the right and left of the Grand Master, with black rods;
Grand Sword Bearer with a drawn sword;
Two Stewards with white rods.

The Marshals conduct the procession to the church, or house, where the services are to be performed. When the front of the procession arrives at the door, they halt, open to the right and left, and face inward; while the Grand Master and others, in succession, pass through and enter the house. A platform is erected in front of the pulpit, and provided with seats for the accommodation of the Grand Officers,

The Holy Bible, Square and Compasses, and Book of Constitutions are placed upon a table in front of the Grand Master. The flooring is then spread in the center, upon the platform, covered with white satin or linen, and encompassed by the three tapers, and the vessels of *corn, wine* and *oil.*

SERVICES.

1. A piece of Music.
2. Prayer.
3. An Oration.
4. A piece of Music.
5. The Grand Marshal forms the officers and members of the new Lodge in front of the Grand Master. The Deputy Grand Master addresses the Grand Master as follows:

MOST WORSHIPFUL:—A number of brethren duly instructed in the mysteries of masonry, having assembled together at stated periods, by virtue of a dispensation granted them for that purpose, do now desire to be *constituted* into a *regular Lodge,* agreeably to the ancient usages and customs of the fraternity.

The dispensation and records are presented to the Grand Master, who examines the records, and, if found correct, proclaims:—

The records appear to be correct and are approved. Upon due deliberation, the Grand Lodge have granted the brethren of this new Lodge a charter, establishing and confirming them in the rights aud privileges of a *regularly constituted Lodge*, which the Grand Secretary will now read.

After the charter is read, the Grand Master then says:—

We shall now proceed, according to ancient usage, to constitute these brethren into a regular Lodge.

Whereupon the several officers of the new Lodge deliver up their jewels and badges to the Master, who presents them, with his own, to the Deputy Grand Master, and he to the Grand Master.

The Deputy Grand Master presents the Master elect to the Grand Master, saying,

Most Worshipful Grand Master:—I present my worthy Brother A. B. to be installed Master of this (new) Lodge. I find him to be of good morals and great skill, true and trusty; and as he is a lover of our whole fraternity, wheresoever dispersed over the face of the earth, I doubt not that he will discharge his duty with fidelity.

The Grand Master asks them if they remain satisfied with their choice. [*They bow in token of assent.*]

The Master elect then presents severally, his wardens and other officers, naming them and their respective offices. The Grand Master asks the brethren if they remain satisfied with each and all of them. [*They bow as before.*]

The officers and members of the new Lodge form in front of the Grand Master; and the business of *consecration* commences with solemn music.

6. CEREMONY OF CONSECRATION.

The Grand Master, attended by the Grand Officers and the Grand Chaplain, form themselves in order round the Lodge—all devoutly kneeling.

7. A piece of solemn music is performed while the Lodge is uncovered.

After which, the first clause of the Consecration Prayer is rehearsed by the Grand Chaplain, which is as follows:

"Great Architect of the Universe! Maker and Ruler of all worlds! deign, from thy celestial temple, from realms of light and glory, to bless us in all the purposes of our present assembly. We humbly invoke thee to give us at this, and at all times, *wisdom* in all our doings, *strength* of mind in all our difficulties, and the *beauty* of harmony in all our communications. Permit us, O thou Author of light and life, great source of love and happiness, to erect this Lodge, and now solemnly to *consecrate* it to the honor of thy glory.

"Glory be to God on high."

[*Response by the brethren.*]

"As it was in the beginning, is now, and ever shall be; world without end. Amen. So mote it be."

The Deputy Grand Master takes the golden Vessel of Corn, and the Senior and Junior Grand Wardens take the Silver Vessels of Wine and Oil, and sprinkle the elements of consecration upon the Lodge.

[The Grand Chaplain then continues:]

"Grant, O Lord our God, that those who are now about to be invested with the government of this Lodge, may be endued with wisdom to instruct their brethren in all their duties. May *brotherly love, relief,* and *truth,* always prevail among the members of this Lodge; and may this bond of union continue to strengthen the Lodges throughout the world.

"Bless all our brethren, wherever dispersed; and grant speedy relief to all who are either oppressed or distressed.

"We affectionately commend to thee, all the members of thy whole family. May they increase in grace, in the knowledge of thee, and in the love of each other.

"Finally: may we finish all our work here below with thy approbation; and then have our transition from this earthly abode to thy heavenly temple above, there to enjoy light, glory and bliss, ineffable and eternal!

"Glory be to God on high."

[*Response by the brethren.*]

"As it was in the beginning, is now, and ever shall be; world without end. Amen."

8. A piece of solemn music is performed while the Carpet is covered.

9. The Grand Chaplain then dedicates the Lodge in the following terms:

"To the memory of the HOLY STS. JOHN, we dedicate this Lodge. May every brother revere their character, and imitate their virtues.

"Glory be to God on high."

[*Response.*]

"As it was in the beginning, is now, and ever shall be; world without end. Amen. So mote it be."

10. A piece of music is performed, while the brethren of the new Lodge advance in procession to salute the Grand Lodge, with their hands crossed upon their breasts as they pass. They then take their places as they were.

11. The Grand Master then rises and constitutes the new Lodge in the form following:

"In the name of the Most Worshipful Grand Lodge, I now constitute and form you, my beloved brethren, into a regular Lodge of free and accepted Masons. From henceforth I empower you to meet as a regular Lodge, constituted in conformity to the rites of our order, and the charges of our ancient and honorable fraternity;—and may the Supreme Architect of the Universe prosper, direct and counsel you in all your doings. Amen."

[*Response.*] "So mote it be."

Section Second.

CEREMONY OF INSTALLATION.

The Grand Master, or presiding officer, addresses the Master elect in the words following, viz:

Brother:—Previous to your investiture, it is necessary that you should signify your assent to those ancient charges and regulations, which point out the duty of a Master of a Lodge.

I. You agree to be a good man and true, and strictly to obey the moral law.

II. You agree to be a peaceable citizen, and cheerfully to conform to the laws of the country in which you reside.

III. You promise not to be concerned in plots and conspiracies against government; but patiently submit to the decisions of the supreme legislature.

IV. You agree to pay a proper respect to the civil magistrates, to work diligently, live creditably, and act honorably by all men.

V. You agree to hold in veneration the original rulers and patrons of the order of masonry, and their regular successors, supreme and subordinate, according to their stations; and to submit to the awards and resolutions of your brethren, when convened in every case consistent with the Constitutions of the order.

VI. You agree to avoid private piques and quarrels, and to guard against intemperance and excess.

VII. You agree to be cautious in carriage, and behaviour, courteous to your brethren, and faithful to your Lodge.

VIII. You promise to respect genuine brethren, and to discountenance imposters, and all dissenters from the original plan of masonry.

IX. You agree to promote the general good of society, to cultivate the social virtues, and to propagate the knowledge of the art.

X. You promise to pay homage to the Grand Master

for the time being, and to his officers when duly installed; and strictly to conform to every edict of the Grand Lodge, or general assembly of Masons, that is not subversive of the principles and ground-work of masonry.

XI. You admit, that it is not in the power of any man, or body of men, to make innovations in the body of masonry.

XII. You promise a regular attendance on the committees and communications of the Grand Lodge, on receiving proper notice, and to pay attention to all the duties of masonry, on convenient occasions.

XIII. You admit that no new Lodge shall be formed without permission of the Grand Lodge; and that no countenance be given to an irregular Lodge, or to any person clandestinely initiated therein, being contrary to the ancient charges of the order.

XIV. You admit that no person can be regularly made a Mason in, or admitted a member of, any regular Lodge, without previous notice, and due inquiry into his character.

XV. You agree that no visiters shall be received into your Lodge, without due examination, and producing proper vouchers of their having been initiated in a regular Lodge.

These are the regulations of free and accepted Masons.

Do you submit to these charges, and promise to support these regulations, as Masters have done in all ages before you?

The Master is to answer, *I do.*

The presiding officer then addresses him:

Brother A. B.:—In consequence of your cheerful conformity to the charges and regulations of the order, you are now to be installed Master of this* Lodge, in full confidence of your care, skill, and capacity to govern the same.

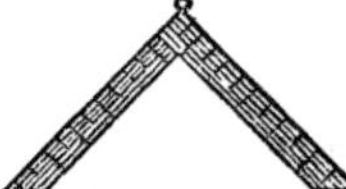

[The new Master is then regularly invested with the insignia of his office, and the furniture and implements of the Lodge.]

The various implements of the profession are emblematical of our conduct in life, and upon this occasion are carefully enumerated.

The *Holy Writings*, that great light in masonry, will guide you to all truth: it will direct your paths to the temple of happiness, and point out to you the whole duty of man.

The *Square* teaches us to regulate our actions by the rule and line, and harmonize our conduct by the principles of morality and virtue.

The *Compasses* teach us to limit our desires in every station; that, rising to eminence by merit, we may live respected and die regretted.

The *Rule* directs that we should punctually observe

---

* If the Lodge is installed for the first time, it is called "This new Lodge."

our duty; press forward in the path of virtue, and neither inclining to the right nor to the left, in all our actions have eternity in view.

The *Line* teaches the criterion of moral rectitude, to avoid dissimulation in conversation and action, and to direct our steps to the path which leads to a glorious immortality.

The *Book of Constitutions* you are to search at all times. Cause it to be read in your Lodge, that none may pretend ignorance of the excellent precepts it enjoins.

You will also receive in charge the *By-laws* of your Lodge, which you are to see carefully and punctually executed.

The subordinate officers are then severally invested by the presiding officer, who delivers each of them a short charge as follows, viz:

The Senior Warden.

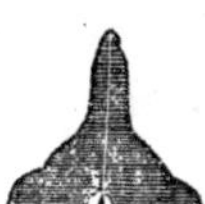

Brother C. D.: You are elected Senior Warden of this Lodge, and are now invested with the badge of your office.

The *level* demonstrates that we are descended from

the same stock, partake of the same nature, and share the same hope; and though distinctions among men are necessary to preserve subordination, yet no eminence of station should make us forget that we are brethren; for he who is placed on the lowest spoke of fortune's wheel, may be entited to our regard; because a time will come, and the wisest knows not how soon, when all distinctions but that of goodness shall cease, and death, the grand leveller of human greatness, reduce us to the same state.

Your regular attendance on our stated meetings, is essentially necessary. In the absence of the Master, you are to govern the Lodge; in his presence you are to assist him in the government of it. I firmly rely on your knowledge of masonry and attachment to the Lodge for the faithful discharge of the duties of this important trust.—*Look well to the West!*

The Junior Warden.

Brother E. F.:—You are elected Junior Warden of this Lodge, and are now invested with the badge of your office. To you, with such assistance as may be necessary, is entrusted the examination of visiters and the preparation of candidates.

The *plumb* admonishes us to walk uprightly in our several stations; to hold the scales of justice in equal poise; and to make our passions and prejudices coincide with the line of duty.

To you is committed the superintendence of the craft, during the hours of refreshment;—it is therefore indispensably necessary, that you should not only be temperate and discreet, in the indulgence of your own inclinations, but carefully observe that none of the craft be suffered to convert the purposes of refreshment into intemperance and excess.

Your regular and punctual attendance is particularly requested; and I have no doubt that you will faithfully execute the duty which you owe to your present appointment.—*Look well to the South!*

The Treasurer.

Brother G. H.:—You are elected Treasurer of this Lodge. It is your duty to receive all moneys from the hands of the Secretary, make due entries of the same, and pay them out by order of the Worshipful Master and the consent of the Lodge.

I trust your regard for the fraternity will prompt you to the faithful discharge of the duties of your office.

The Secretary.

Brother J. K.:—You are elected Secretary of this Lodge. It is your duty to observe all the proceedings of the Lodge; make a fair record of all things proper to be written; to receive all moneys paid to the Lodge, and pay them over to the Treasurer, and take his receipt for the same.

Your good inclination to masonry and this Lodge, I hope, will induce you to discharge the duties of your office with fidelity; and by so doing, you will merit the esteem and applause of your brethren.

Senior and Junior Deacons.

Brothers L. M. and N. O.:—You are elected Deacons of this Lodge. It is your province to attend on the Master and Wardens, and to act as their proxies in the active duties of the Lodge; such as in the reception of candidates into the different degrees of masonry, and in the immediate practice of our rites. The *Square* and *Compasses*, as badges of your office, I entrust to your care, not doubting your vigilance and attention.

The Stewards.

BROTHERS P. Q. AND R. S.:—You are elected Stewards of this Lodge. The duties of your office are, to assist in the collection of dues and subscriptions; to keep an account of the Lodge expenses; and generally to assist the deacons and other officers in performing their duties.

Your regular and early attendance will afford the best proof of your zeal and attachment to the Lodge.

The Tyler.

BROTHER:—You are elected Tyler of this Lodge, and I invest you with the implement of your office. As the sword is placed in the hands of the Tyler, to enable him effectually to guard against the approach of cowans and eves-droppers, and suffer none to pass or repass but such as are duly qualified; so it should morally serve as a constant admonition to us, to set a guard at the entrance of our thoughts; to place a watch at the door of our lips; and to post a sentinel over our actions: thereby excluding every unqualified and unworthy thought, word and deed; and preserving consciences void of offence towards God and towards man.

Your early and punctual attendance will afford the best proof of your zeal for the institution.

CHARGE upon the Installation of the Master of a Lodge.

Worshipful Master—Being elected Master of this Lodge, you cannot be insensible of the obligations which devolve on you, as its head; nor of your responsibility for the faithful discharge of the important duties annexed to your station.

The honor, reputation, and usefulness of your Lodge, will materially depend on the skill and assiduity with which you manage its concerns; while the happiness of its members will be generally promoted, in proportion to the zeal and ability with which you propagate the genuine principles of our institution.

For a pattern of imitation, consider the great luminary of nature, which, rising in the *East,* regularly diffuses light and lustre to all within its circle. In like manner, it is your province to spread and communicate light and instruction to the brethren of your Lodge. Forcibly impress upon them the dignity and high importance of masonry, and seriously admonish them never to disgrace it.—Charge them to practice out of the Lodge, those duties which are taught in it; and by amiable, discreet, and virtuous conduct, to convince mankind of the goodness of the institution; so that, when any one is said to be a member of it, the world may know that he is one to whom the burthened heart may pour out its sorrows; to whom distress may prefer its suit; whose hand is guided by justice, and whose heart is expanded by benevolence. In short, by a diligent observance of the By-laws of your Lodge, the

Constitutions of masonry, and, above all, the *Holy Scriptures,* which are given as a rule and guide to your faith and practice, you will be enabled to acquit yourself with honor and reputation, and lay up a *crown* of *rejoicing,* which shall continue when time shall be no more.

CHARGE to Senior and Junior Wardens.

BROTHER SENIOR AND JUNIOR WARDENS—You are too well acquainted with the principles of masonry to warrant any distrust that you will be found wanting in the discharge of your respective duties.—Suffice it to mention, that what you have seen praiseworthy in others, you should carefully imitate; and what in them may have appeared defective, you should in yourselves amend. You should be examples for good order and regularity; for it is only by a due regard to the laws in your own conduct, that you can expect obedience to them from others. You are assiduously to assist the Master in the discharge of his trust; diffusing light and imparting knowledge to all whom he shall place under your care. In the absence of the Master you will succeed to higher duties; your acquirements must therefore be such, as that the Craft may never suffer for want of proper instruction. From the spirit which you have hitherto evinced, I entertain no doubt that your future conduct will be such as to merit the applause of your brethren, and the testimony of a good conscience.

BRETHREN OF ——— LODGE—Such is the nature of our Constitution, that as some must of necessity rule and teach, so others must of course learn to submit and obey. Humility in both is an essential duty. The officers who are appointed to govern your Lodge, are sufficiently conversant with the rules of propriety, and the laws of the institution, to avoid exceeding the powers with which they are entrusted; and you are of too generous dispositions to envy their preferment. I therefore trust that you will have but one aim, to please each other, and unite in the grand design of being happy, and communicating happiness.

Finally, my brethren, as this association has been formed and perfected with so much unanimity and concord, in which we greatly rejoice, so may it long continue. May you long enjoy every satisfaction and delight which disinterested friendship can afford. May kindness and brotherly affection distinguish your conduct, as men, and as Masons. Within your peaceful walls, may your children's children celebrate with joy and gratitude, the transactions of this auspicious solemnity. And may *the tenets of our profession* be transmitted through your Lodge, pure and unimpaired, from generation to generation.

12. The Grand Marshal then proclaims the new Lodge in the following manner, viz:

In the name of the Most Worshipful Grand Lodge of the State of ———, I proclaim this new Lodge by the name of ——— Lodge, No. —, to be legally constituted, consecrated, and the officers thereof duly installed.

13. A piece of music is then performed.

14. Benediction.

The Grand Officers being seated, all but Master Masons are caused to retire.

A procession is then formed, and passes three times round the hall; and upon passing the Master, pays him due homage by the usual honors, in the different degrees.

While the procession is passing round, the following song is sung:

HAIL MASONRY divine!
Glory of ages shine;
  Long may'st thou reign;
Where'er thy lodges stand,
May they have great command,
And always grace the land,
  Thou Art divine;

Great fabrics still arise,
And grace the azure skies;
  Great are thy schemes;
Thy noble orders are
Matchless, beyond compare;
No art with thee can share,
  Thou Art divine.

Hiram, the Architect,
Did all the Craft direct
  How they should build:

Sol'mon, great Israel's king,
Did mighty blessings bring,
And left us room to sing,
  Hail, royal Art! } Chorus three times.

The Grand Master then directs the Grand Marshal to form the procession; when the Grand Lodge walk to their own hall, and both Lodges are closed in due form.

Section Third.

This section contains the ceremony observed on laying the foundation stones of public structures.

This ceremony is conducted by the M. W. Grand Master and his officers, assisted by such officers and members of subordinate Lodges, as can conveniently attend. The chief magistrate, and other civil officers of the place where the building is to be erected, also generally attend on the occasion.

At the time appointed, the Grand Lodge is convened in some suitable place. A band of martial music is provided, and the brethren appear in the insignia of the Order.

The Lodge is then opened by the Grand Master, and the rules for regulating the procession are read by the Grand Secretary. The Lodge is then adjourned; after which the procession sets out in *due form,* in the following order:

Procession at laying Foundation Stones.

Two Tylers with drawn Swords;
Tyler of the oldest Lodge with a drawn Sword;

Two Stewards of the oldest Lodge;
Entered Apprentices;
Fellow Crafts;
Master Masons;
Past Secretaries;
Past Treasurers;
Past Junior Wardens;
Past Senior Wardens;
Mark Masters;
Past Masters;
Royal Arch Masons;
Select Masters;
Knights Templars;
Masters;
Music;

Marshal.

Grand Tyler with a drawn Sword;
Grand Stewards with white Rods;
A Past Master with a Golden Vessel containing Corn;
Principal Architect with Square, Level and Plumb;
Two Past Masters with Silver Vessels, one containing Wine, and the other Oil;
Grand Secretary and Treasurer;
The Five Orders;
One large light borne by a Past Master;
The Holy Bible, Square and Compasses, borne by a Master of a Lodge, supported by two Stewards on the right and left;
Two large Lights, borne by two Past Masters;
Grand Chaplain;

Clergy and Orator;
Grand Wardens;
Deputy Grand Master;
The Master of the oldest Lodge, carrying the Book of Constitutions on a velvet cushion;
Grand Deacons with black Rods, on a line Seven feet apart;
Grand Master;
Two Stewards with white rods;
Grand Sword Bearer with a drawn Sword.

A Triumphal Arch is usually erected at the place where the ceremony is to be performed. The procession passes through the arch; and the brethren repairing to their stands, the Grand Master and his officers take their places on a temporary platform, covered with carpet. The Grand Master commands silence. An Ode on Masonry is sung; after which, the necessary preparations are made for laying the stone, on which is engraved the year of masonry, the name and title of the Grand Master, &c., &c.

The stone is raised up by means of an engine erected for that purpose, and the Grand Chaplain or Orator repeats a short prayer.

The Grand Treasurer, then, by the Grand Master's command, places under the stone various sorts of coin and medals of the present age. Solemn music is introduced, and the stone is let down into its place.

The principal architect then presents the working tools to the Grand Master, who applies the *plumb, square* and *level* to the stone, in their proper position, and pronounces it to be WELL FORMED, TRUE, and TRUSTY.

The golden and silver vessels are next brought to the table and delivered; the former to the Deputy Grand Master, and the latter to the Grand Wardens, who successively present them to the Grand Master; and he, according to ancient ceremony, pours the corn, the wine and the oil, which they contain, on the stone; saying—

"May the all-bounteous Author of Nature bless the inhabitants of this place with all the necessaries, conveniences and comforts of this life; assist in the erection and completion of this building; protect the workmen against every accident, and long preserve this structure from decay; and grant to us all, a supply of the CORN of *nourishment*, the WINE of *refreshment*, and the OIL of *joy!*

"Amen. So mote it be."

He then strikes the stone thrice with the mallet; and the *public grand honors are given.* The Grand Master then delivers over to the Architect the various implements of architecture, entrusting him with the superintendence and direction of the work; after which, he re-ascends the platform, and an oration suitable to the occasion is delivered.

A voluntary collection is made for the needy workmen; and the sum collected is placed upon the stone by the Grand Treasurer.

A suitable song in honor of masonry concludes the ceremony; after which, the procession returns to the place whence it set out, and the Lodge is closed in due form.

Section Fourth.

The fourth section contains the ceremony observed at the Dedication of Freemasons' Halls.

On the day appointed, the Grand Master and his officers, accompanied by the members of the Grand Lodge, meet in a convenient room near the place where the ceremony is to be performed, and open in *due and ample form,* in the third degree of masonry.

The Master of the Lodge, to which the Hall to be dedicated belongs, being present, addresses the Grand Master as follows:

MOST WORSHIPFUL—The brethren of ——— Lodge, being animated with a desire of promoting the honor and interest of the craft, have, at great pains and expense, erected a masonic Hall for their convenience and accommodation. They are now desirous that the same should be examined by the M. W. GRAND LODGE, and if it meet their approbation, that it should be solemnly dedicated to masonic purposes, agreeably to *ancient form.*

The Grand Master then directs the Grand Marshal to form the procession, when they move forward to the Hall to be dedicated. On entering, the music will continue while the procession marches three times round the Hall.

The carpet, or flooring, is then placed in the center; and the Grand Master having taken the chair, under a canopy of state, the Grand Officers, and the Masters and Wardens of the Lodge, repair to the places previously prepared for their reception. The three Lights, and the Golden and Silver Pitchers, with the corn, wine and oil, are placed round the Lodge, at the head of which stands the Altar, with the Holy Bible open, and the Square and Compasses laid thereon, with the Charter, Book of Constitutions, and By-laws.

An Anthem is sung, and an Exordium on masonry given; after which, the Architect addresses the Grand Master, as follows:

MOST WORSHIPFUL—Having been entrusted with the superintendence and management of the workmen employed in the erection of this edifice; and having, according to the best of my ability, accomplished the task assigned me, I now return my thanks for the honor of this appointment, and beg leave to surrender up the implements which were committed to my care when the foundation of this fabric was laid; humbly hoping that the exertions which have been made on this occasion, will be crowned with your approbation, and that of the Most Worshipful Grand Lodge.

To which the Grand Master makes the following reply:

BROTHER ARCHITECT—The skill and fidelity displayed in the execution of the trust reposed in you at the commencement of this undertaking, have secured the approbation of the Grand Lodge; and they sincerely pray, that this edifice may continue a lasting monument of the taste, spirit, and liberality of its founders.

An Ode in honor of masonry is sung, accompanied with instrumental music.

The Deputy Grand Master then rises and says:

Most Worshipful—The Hall in which we are now assembled, and the plan upon which it has been constructed, having met with your approbation, it is the desire of the fraternity that it should now be dedicated according to ancient form and usage.

Whereupon a procession is formed in the following order, viz:

Grand Sword Bearer;
A Past Master with a Light;
A Past Master with a Bible, Square, and Compasses, on a velvet cushion;
Two Past Masters each with a Light;
Grand Secretary and Treasurer with Emblems;
Junior Grand Warden with Pitcher of Corn;
Senior Grand Warden with Pitcher of Wine;
Deputy Grand Master with Pitcher of Oil;
Grand Master;
Two Stewards with Rods.

All the other brethren keep their places and assist in performing an Ode, which continues during the procession, excepting only at the intervals of dedication. The Carpet being uncovered, the first time passing round it the Grand Junior Warden presents the pitcher of Corn to the Grand Master, who pours it out upon the Lodge, at the same time pronouncing—

"In the name of the Great JEHOVAH, to whom be all honor and glory, I do solemnly dedicate this Hall to MASONRY."

The grand honors are given.

The second time passing round the Lodge, the Senior Grand Warden presents the pitcher of Wine to the Grand Master, who sprinkles it upon the Carpet, at the same time saying—

"In the name of the HOLY SAINTS JOHN, I do solemnly dedicate this Hall to VIRTUE."

The grand honors are twice given.

The third time passing round the Lodge, the Deputy Grand Master presents the Grand Master with the pitcher of Oil, who pours it upon the Carpet, saying—

"In the name of the whole Fraternity, I do solemnly dedicate this Hall to UNIVERSAL BENEVOLENCE."

The grand honors are thrice given.

A solemn Invocation is made to the Throne of Grace by the Grand Chaplain, and an Anthem sung; after which the Carpet is covered, and the Grand Master retires to his Chair.

An Oration is then delivered, and the ceremonies conclude with music. The Grand Lodge is then closed in due or ample form.

Section Fifth.

This section contains the ceremony observed at

Funerals, according to the ancient custom; together with the service used on such occasions.

No Mason can be interred with the formalities of the order, unless it be by his own special request, foreigners and sojourners excepted; nor unless he has been raised to the sublime degree of Master Mason; as no Fellow Craft or Entered Apprentice is entitled to funeral obsequies, nor to attend the masonic procession on such occasions.

All the brethren who walk in procession, should observe, as much as possible, an uniformity in their dress. Decent mourning around the left arm, with white gloves and aprons, are most suitable.

THE FUNERAL SERVICE.

The brethren being assembled at the Lodge-room, (or some other convenient place,) the presiding officer opens the Lodge in the third degree, with the usual forms; and having stated the purpose of the meeting, the service begins:

Master. "What man is he that liveth, and shall not see death? Shall he deliver his soul from the hand of the grave?"

Response. "Man walketh in a vain shadow; he heapeth up riches, and cannot tell who shall gather them."

Master. "When he dieth he shall carry nothing away; his glory shall not descend after him."

Response. "Naked he came into the world, and naked he must return."

Master. "The Lord gave and the Lord hath taken away; blessed be the name of the Lord."

The Master then taking the roll in his hand, says—

"Let us live and die like the righteous, and our last end shall be like his!"

The Brethren answer—"God is our God forever and ever; he will be our guide even unto death!"

The Master then records the name and age of the deceased upon the *roll*, and says—

"Almighty Father! in thy hands we leave, with humble submission, the soul of our deceased brother."

The brethren answer three times—

"The will of God is accomplished! So be it."

The Master then deposits the *roll* in the *archives*, and repeats the following Prayer:

"Most glorious God! author of all good, and giver of all mercy, pour down thy blessings upon us, and strengthen our solemn engagements with the ties of sincere affection! May the present instance of mortality remind us of our approaching fate, and draw our attention toward thee, the only refuge in time of need; that when the awful moment shall arrive, when we are about to quit this transitory scene, the enlivening prospect of thy mercy may dispel the gloom of death; and after our departure hence in peace, and in thy favor, may we be received into thy everlasting kingdom, to enjoy, in union with the souls of our departed friends, the just reward of a pious and virtuous life. Amen."

A procession is then formed, which moves to the house of the deceased, and thence to the place of interment.

Order of Procession at a Funeral.

Tyler with a drawn sword;
Stewards with white rods;
Musicians, (if they are Masons, otherwise they precede the Tyler;)
Master Masons;
Senior and Junior Deacons;
Secretary and Treasurer;
Senior and Junior Wardens;
Mark Masters;
Past Masters;
Royal Arch Masons;
Select Masters;
Knights Templars;
The Holy Writings on a cushion, covered with black cloth, carried by the oldest (or some suitable) member of the Lodge;
The Master;
Clergy;
The Body, with the insignia placed thereon.

Marshal;

Pall Bearers. Pall Bearers.

When the procession arrives at the church-yard, the members of the Lodge form a circle round the grave; and the clergyman and officers of the Lodge take their station at the head of the grave, and the mourners at the foot. The service is resumed, and the following Exhortation is given by the Master:

"BRETHREN—Here we view a striking instance of the uncertainty of life, and the vanity of all human pursuits. The last offices paid to the dead, are only useful as lectures to the living;—from them we are to derive instruction, and to consider every solemnity of this kind as a summons to prepare for our approaching dissolution.

"Notwithstanding the various mementos of mortality with which we daily meet; notwithstanding Death has established his empire over all the works of nature; yet, through some unaccountable infatuation, we forget that we are born to die; we go on from one design to another, add hope to hope, and lay our plans for the employment of many years, till we are suddenly alarmed with the approach of Death when we least expect him, and at an hour which we probably conclude to be the meridian of our existence.

"What are all the externals of majesty, the pride of wealth, or charms of beauty, when Nature has paid her just debt? Fix your eyes on the last scene, and view life stript of her ornaments and exposed in her natural meanness; you will then be convinced of the futility of those empty delusions. In the grave all fallacies are detected, all ranks are leveled, and all distinctions are done away.

"When we view this narrow house, about to be occupied by the body of our deceased brother, we feel a momentary contraction of the heart, a mournful presage that here, too, the evening of our days must soon be closed, and the tear of affection that trembles to-day upon another's tomb must soon be transferred to ours. These become strong incentives to a well regulated life; and when the whispers of conscience plead in vain with our unsubdued passions, the grave, that universal monitor, informs us this must be our final destination.

"While we drop the sympathetic tear over the grave of our deceased friend, let charity incline us to throw a veil over his foibles, whatever they may have been, and not withhold from his memory the praise that his virtues may have claimed. Suffer the apologies of human nature to plead in his behalf. Perfection on earth has never been attained; the wisest, as well as the best of men, have erred.

"Let the present example excite our most serious thoughts, and strengthen our resolutions of amendment. As life is uncertain, and all earthly pursuits are vain, let us no longer postpone the all-important concern of preparing for eternity; but embrace the happy moment, while time and opportunity offer, to provide against the great change, when all the pleasures of this world shall cease to delight, and the reflections of a virtuous and holy life yield the only comfort and consolation. Thus our expectations will not be frustrated, nor we hurried unprepared into the presence of an all-wise and powerful Judge, to whom the secrets of all hearts are known.

"Let us, while in this state of existence, support with propriety the character of our profession, advert to the nature of our solemn ties, and pursue with assiduity the sacred tenets of our order. Then, with becoming reverence, let us seek the favor of the ETERNAL GOD, so that when the awful moment of death arrives, be it soon or late, we may be enabled to prosecute our journey without dread or apprehension, to that far distant country, whence no traveller returns."

The following invocations are then made by the Master:

Master. "May we be true and faithful, and may we live and die in love!"

Response. "So mote it be."

Master. "May we profess what is good, and always act agreeably to our profession!"

Response. "So mote it be."

Master. "May the Lord bless us and prosper us, and may all our good intentions be crowned with success!"

Response. "So mote it be."

Master. "Glory be to God in the highest; on earth peace! good will towards men!"

Response. "So mote it be, now, from henceforth, and for evermore. Amen.

The apron is taken off from the coffin and handed to the Master—the coffin is deposited in the grave—and the Master says:

This Lamb skin, or white Apron, is an emblem of Innocence and the badge of a Mason, more ancient than the golden fleece or Roman eagle; and when worthily worn, more honorable than the star and garter. [*The Master then deposits it in the grave.*] This emblem I now deposit in the grave of our deceased Brother. By this we are reminded of the universal dominion of Death. The arm of friendship cannot oppose the King of Terrors, nor the charms of innocence elude his grasp. This grave, that coffin, this circle of mourning friends, remind us that we too are mortal: soon shall our bodies moulder to dust. Then how important for us that we should know that our REDEEMER liveth, and that he shall stand at the latter day upon the Earth. [*The Master, holding the evergreen in his hand, continues.*] This *evergreen* is an emblem of our faith in the immortality of the soul. By this we are reminded that we have an immortal part within us which shall survive the grave, and which shall never, never, never die. Though like our Brother, whose remains now lie before us, we shall soon be clothed in the habiliments of DEATH and be deposited in the silent tomb, yet through the mediation of a divine and ascended Saviour, we may confidently hope that our souls will bloom in Eternal Spring.

The brethren then move in procession round the place of interment, and severally drop the sprig of evergreen into the grave; after which, *the public grand honors are given.*

The Master then continues the ceremony at the grave, in the following words:

"FRIENDS AND FELLOW CITIZENS:—From time immemorial it has been the custom among the Fraternity of Free and Accepted Masons, at the request of a brother, to accompany his corpse to the place of interment, and there to deposit his remains with the usual formalities.

"In conformity to this usage, and at the special request of our deceased brother, whose memory we revere, and whose loss we now deplore, we have assembled in the character of Masons, to resign his body to the earth whence it came, and to offer up to his memory, before the world, the last tribute of our affection; thereby demonstrating the sincerity of our past esteem, and our steady attachment to the principles of the Order.

"The Great Creator having been pleased, out of his mercy, to remove our brother from the cares and troubles of a transitory existence, to a state of eternal duration, and thereby to weaken the chain by which we are united man to man; may we who survive him, anticipate our approaching fate, and be more strongly cemented in the ties of union and friendship; that, during the short space allotted to our present existence, we may wisely and usefully employ our time; and, in the reciprocal intercourse of kind and friendly acts, mutually promote the welfare and happiness of each other.

"Unto the grave we resign the body of our deceased friend, there to remain until the general resurrection, in favorable expectation that his immortal soul may partake of joys which have been prepared for the righteous from the beginning of the world. And may Almighty God, of his infinite goodness, at the grand tribunal of unbiassed justice, extend his mercy towards him, and all of us, and crown our hope with everlasting bliss in the expanded realms of a boundless eternity! This we beg, for the honor of his name; to whom be glory, now and forever. Amen."

The procession then returns in form to the place whence it set out, where the necessary duties are complied with, and the Lodge is closed in the third degree.

NOTE. *If the Grand Master attends, and presides at any ceremony, it is said to be performed in* AMPLE FORM; *if a subordinate officer in the Grand Lodge, in* DUE FORM; *if vested in the Master of a subordinate Lodge, in* FORM.

CHAPTER III.

MOST EXCELLENT MASTER'S DEGREE.

None but the meritorious and praiseworthy; none but those who, through diligence and industry, have progressed far towards perfection and *passed the chair*, can be admitted to this degree of masonry.

When the temple of Jerusalem was finished, and the cap-stone celebrated with great joy, King Solomon admitted to this degree only those who had proved themselves worthy, by their virtue, skill, and inflexible fidelity to the Craft. The duties incumbent on a Most Excellent Master are such, that he should have a perfect knowledge of all the preceding degrees.

The following Psalm is read at opening:

"The earth is the Lord's, and the fulness thereof; the world, and they that dwell therein. For he hath founded it upon the seas, and established it upon the floods. Who shall ascend into the hill of the Lord? or who shall stand in his holy place? He that hath clean hands and a pure heart; who hath not lifted up his soul unto vanity, nor sworn deceitfully. He shall receive the blessing from the Lord, and righteousness from the God of his salvation. This is the generation of them that seek him, that seek thy face, O Jacob: Selah. Lift up your heads, O ye gates: and be ye lift up, ye everlasting doors, and the King of Glory shall come in. Who is this King of Glory? The Lord strong and mighty, the Lord mighty in battle. Lift up your heads, O ye gates; even lift them up, ye everlasting doors, and the King of Glory shall come in. Who is this King of Glory? The Lord of Hosts, he is the King of Glory. Selah."—*Psalm* xxiv.

The following Psalm is read during the ceremony of receiving a candidate in this degree:

"I was glad when they said unto me, Let us go into the house of the Lord. Our feet shall stand within thy gates, O Jerusalem. Jerusalem is builded as a city that is compact together: whither the tribes go up, the tribes of the Lord, unto the testimony of Israel, to give thanks unto the name of the Lord. For there are set thrones of judgment, the thrones of the house of David.

"Pray for the peace of Jerusalem: they shall prosper that love thee. Peace be within thy walls, and prosperity within thy palaces. For my brethren and companions' sakes, I will now say, Peace be within thee. Because of the house of the Lord our God, I will seek thy good."—*Psalm* cxxii.

The following song is sung with solemn ceremony:

MOST EXCELLENT MASTER'S SONG.

Cres.
The cap-stone is finish'd, Our la - bor is o'er;
The capstone is finish'd, Our lab - or is o'er;
The sound of the ga-vel shall hail us no more.
The sound of the ga-vel shall hail us no more.
For.
To the Pow-er Al-migh-ty, who ev-er has gui - ded
To the Pow-er Al-migh-ty, who ev-er has gui - ded

The tribes of old Is - rael, ex - alt - ing their fame;
The tribes of old Is - rael, ex - alt - ing their fame;
To Him, who hath govern'd our hearts un - di-vided,
To Him, who hath govern'd our hearts un - di-vided,
Fortiss.
Let's send forth our voi-ces to praise his great Name.
Let's send forth our voi-ces to praise his great Name.

Companions assemble
  On this joyful day;
The occasion is glorious,
  The key-stone to lay:
Fulfill'd is the promise,
  By the ANCIENT OF DAYS,
To bring forth the cap-stone
  With shouting and praise.

[*Ceremonies.*]

There is no more occasion for level or plumb-line,
For trowel or gavel, for compass or square:
Our works are completed, the ark safely seated,
And we shall be greeted as workmen most rare.

Now those who are worthy,
  Our toils who have shar'd,
And prov'd themselves faithful,
  Shall meet their reward;
Their virtue and knowledge,
  Industry and skill,
Have our approbation,
  Have gain'd our good will.

We accept and receive them, Most Excellent Masters,
Invested with honors, and power to preside;
Among worthy crafts-men, wherever assembled,
The knowledge of Masons to spread far and wide.

ALMIGHTY JEHOVAH!
  Descend now and fill
This Lodge with thy glory,
  Our hearts with good will!

Preside at our meetings,
  Assist us to find
True pleasure in teaching
  Good will to mankind.
Thy *wisdom* inspired the great institution,
Thy *strength* shall support it till nature expire;
And when the creation shall fall into ruin,
Its *beauty* shall rise through the midst of the fire!

The following passages of Scripture are also introduced, accompanied with solemn ceremonies:

Then said Solomon, The Lord hath said that he would dwell in the thick darkness. But I have built a house of habitation for thee, and a place for thy dwelling for ever.

And the king turned his face, and blessed the whole congregation of Israel: and all the congregation of Israel stood. And he said, Blessed be the Lord God of Israel, who hath with his hands fulfilled that which he spake with his mouth to my father David, saying, Since the day that I brought forth my people out of the land of Egypt, I chose no city among all the tribes of Israel to build a house in, that my name might be there; neither chose I any man to be a ruler over my people Israel: but I have chosen Jerusalem, that my name might be there; and have chosen David to be over my people Israel.

Now it was in the heart of David my father to build a house for the name of the Lord God of Israel. But the Lord said to David my father, Forasmuch as it was in thy heart to build a house for my name, thou didst well in that it was in thy heart; notwithstanding, thou shalt not build the house; but thy son which shall come forth out of thy loins, he shall build the house for my name. The Lord therefore hath performed his word that he hath spoken; for I am risen up in the room of David my father, and am set on the throne of Israel, as the Lord promised, and have built the house for the name of the Lord God of Israel. And in it have I put the ark, wherein is the covenant of the Lord, that he made with the children of Israel.

And he stood before the altar of the Lord, in the presence of all the congregation of Israel, and spread forth his hands: (for Solomon had made a brazen scaffold of five cubits long, and five cubits broad, and three cubits high, and had set it in the midst of the court; and upon it he stood, and kneeled down upon his knees before all the congregation of Israel, and spread forth his hands towards heaven,) and said,

O Lord God of Israel, there is no God like thee in the heaven, nor in the earth; which keepest covenant, and shewest mercy unto thy servants that walk before thee with all their hearts: thou which hast kept with thy servant David my father that which thou hast promised him; and spakest with thy mouth, and hast fulfilled it with thine hand, as it is this day. Now therefore, O Lord God of Israel, keep with thy servant David my father that which thou hast promised him, saying, There shall not fail thee a man in my sight to sit upon the throne of Israel; yet so that thy children take heed to their way, to walk in my law, as thou hast walked before me. Now then, O Lord God of Israel, let thy word be verified, which thou hast spoken unto thy servant David. But, will God in very deed dwell with men on the earth? Behold, heaven and the heaven of heavens cannot contain thee; how much less this house which I have built! Have respect therefore to the prayer of thy servant and to his supplication, O Lord my God, to hearken unto the cry and the prayer which thy servant prayeth before thee: that thine eyes may be open upon this house day and night, upon the place whereof thou hast said that thou wouldst put thy name there; to hearken unto the prayer which thy servant prayeth towards this place.

Hearken therefore unto the supplications of thy servant, and of thy people Israel, which they shall make toward this place: hear thou from thy dwelling place, even from heaven; and when thou hearest, forgive.

Now when Solomon had made an end of praying, the fire came down from heaven, and consumed the burnt-offering and the sacrifices; and the glory of the Lord filled the house. And the priests could not enter into the house of the Lord, because the glory of the Lord had filled the Lord's house.

And when all the children of Israel saw how the fire came down, and the glory of the Lord upon the house, they bowed themselves with their faces to the ground upon the pavement, and worshipped, and praised the Lord, saying, For he is good; for his mercy endureth for ever.—2 *Chronicles* vi. vii.

CHARGE to a Brother who is received and acknowledged as a Most Excellent Master.

BROTHER:—Your admittance to this degree of masonry, is a proof of the good opinion the brethren of this Lodge entertain of your masonic abilities. Let this consideration induce you to be careful of forfeiting, by misconduct and inattention to our rules, that esteem which has raised you to the rank you now possess.

It is one of your great duties as a Most Excellent Master, to dispense light and truth to the uninformed Mason; and I need not remind you of the impossibility of complying with this obligation, without possessing an accurate acquaintance with the lectures of each degree.

If you are not already completely conversant in all the degrees heretofore conferred on you, remember that an indulgence, prompted by a belief that you will apply yourself with double diligence to make yourself so, has induced the brethren to accept you.

Let it therefore be your unremitting study, to acquire such a degree of knowledge and information, as shall enable you to discharge with propriety, the various duties incumbent on you, and to preserve unsullied the title now conferred upon you, of a MOST EXCELLENT MASTER.

The following Psalm is read at closing:

"The Lord is my shepherd; I shall not want. He maketh me to lie down in green pasture: he leadeth me beside the still waters. He restoreth my soul: he leadeth me in the paths of righteousness for his name's sake. Yea, though I walk through the valley of the shadow of death, I will fear no evil: for thou art with me; thy rod and thy staff they comfort me. Thou preparest a table before me in the presence of mine enemies: thou anointest my head with oil; my cup runneth over. Surely goodness and mercy shall follow me all the days of my life: aud I will dwell in the house of the Lord for ever."—*Psalm* xxiii.

CHAPTER IV.

ROYAL ARCH DEGREE.

This degree is more august, sublime and important, than all which precede it. It impresses on our minds a belief of the being and existence of the Supreme Grand High Priest of our Salvation, who is without beginning of days or end of years; and forcibly reminds us of the reverence due his Holy Name.

In this degree is brought to light many essentials which are of importance to the craft, that were concealed in darkness for the space of four hundred and seventy years; and without a knowledge of which, the masonic character cannot be complete.

Section First.

This section explains the mode of government in this degree; it designates the appellation, number and situation of the several officers, and points out the purpose and duty of their respective stations. The various colors of their banners are designated; and the morals to which they allude are introduced and explained.

The following exhortation is read at opening:

"Now we command you, brethren, that ye withdraw yourselves from every brother that walketh disorderly, and not after the tradition which ye received of us. For yourselves know how ye ought to follow us: for we behaved not ourselves disorderly among you; neither did we eat any man's bread for nought; but wrought with labor and travail night and day, that we might not be chargeable to any of you: not because we have not power, but to make ourselves an example unto you to follow us. For even when we were with you, this we commanded you, that if any would not work, neither should he eat. For we hear that there are some which walk among you disorderly, working not at all, but are busy bodies. Now them that are such we command and exhort, that with quietness they work, and eat their own bread. But ye, brethren, be not weary in well-doing. And if any man obey not our word by this epistle, note that man, and have no company with him, that he may be ashamed. Ye count him not as an enemy, but admonish him as a brother. Now the Lord of Peace himself give you peace always by all means. The Lord be with you all.

Section Second.

This section contains much valuable historical information, and exhibits to our view, in striking colors, that prosperity and happiness are ever the ultimate consequences of virtue and justice; while disgrace and ruin invariably follow the practice of vice and immorality.

The following charges and passages of Scripture are introduced during the ceremony of exaltation:

"I will bring the blind by a way they know not; I will lead them in paths that they have not known; I will make darkness light before them, and crooked things straight. These things will I do unto them, and not forsake them."—*Isaiah* xlii. 16.

Prayer used at the exaltation of a Royal Arch Mason.

"O thou eternal and omnipotent JEHOVAH, the glorious and everlasting I AM; permit us, thy frail, dependent and needy creatures, in the name of our *Most Excellent and Supreme High Priest,* to approach thy divine majesty. And do thou, who sittest *between the Cherubim,* incline thine ear to the voice of our praises, and of our supplication; and vouchsafe to commune with us from off the *mercy seat.* We humbly adore and worship thy unspeakable perfections, and thy unbounded goodness and benevolence. We bless thee, that when man had sinned and fallen from his innocence and happiness, thou didst still leave unto him the powers of reasoning, and the capacity of improvement and of pleasure. We adore thee, that amidst the pains and calamities of our present state, so many means of refreshment and satisfaction are afforded us, while travelling the *rugged path of life.* And O, thou who didst aforetime appear unto thy servant Moses *in a flame of fire, out of the midst of a bush,* enkindle, we beseech thee, in each of our hearts, a flame of devotion to thee, of love to each other, and of benevolence and charity to all mankind. May the *veils* of ignorance and blindness be removed from the eyes of our understandings, that we may behold and adore thy mighty and wondrous works. May the *rod* and staff of thy grace and power continually support us, and defend us from the rage of all our enemies, and especially from the subtilty and malice of that old *serpent,* who with cruel vigilance seeketh our ruin. May the *leprosy* of sin be eradicated from our *bosoms;* and may *Holiness to the Lord* be engraven upon all our thoughts, words, and actions. May the *incense* of piety ascend continually unto thee, from off the *altar* of our hearts, and *burn day and night* as a sweet-smelling savor unto thee. May we daily *search* the records of *truth,* that we may be more and more instructed in our duty; and may we share the blessedness of those who hear the *sacred word, and keep it.* And finally, O merciful Father, when we shall have passed through the outward *veils* of these earthly *courts;* when the earthly house of this *tabernacle* shall be dissolved, may we be admitted into the *Holy of Holies* above, into the presence of the Grand Council of heaven, where the Supreme High Priest for ever presides, for ever reigns. Amen. So mote it be."

"Now Moses kept the flock of Jethro his father-in-law, the priest of Midian; and he led the flock to the back side of the desert, and came to the mountain of God, even to Horeb. And the angel of the Lord appeared unto him in a flame of fire, out of the midst of a bush; and he looked, and behold the bush burned with fire, and the bush was not consumed. And Moses said, I will now turn aside, and see this great sight, why the bush is not burnt.

"And when the Lord saw that he turned aside to see, God called unto him out of the midst of the bush, and said Moses, Moses. And he said, Here am I. And he said, Draw not nigh hither; put off thy shoes from off thy feet, for the place whereon thou standest is holy ground. Moreover he said, I am the God of thy father, the God of Abraham, the God of Isaac, and the God of Jacob. And Moses hid his face; for he was afraid to look upon God."—*Exodus* iii. 1–6.

"Zedekiah was one and twenty years old when he began to reign, and reigned eleven years in Jerusalem. And he did that which was evil in the sight of the Lord his God, and humbled not himself before Jeremiah the prophet, speaking from the mouth of the Lord. And he also rebelled against king Nebuchadnezzar: and stiffened his neck, and hardened his heart from turning unto the Lord God of Israel. Moreover, all of the chief of the priests, and the people, transgressed very much after all the abominations of the heathen; and polluted the house of the Lord which he had hallowed in Jerusalem. And the Lord God of their fathers sent to them by his messengers, because he had compassion on his people, and on his dwelling place: But they mocked the messengers of God, and despised his words, and misused his prophets, until the wrath of the Lord arose against his people, till there was no remedy. Therefore he brought upon them the king of the Chaldees, who slew their young men with the sword in the house of their sanctuary, and had no compassion upon young man or maiden, old man, or him that stooped for age: he gave them all into his hand. And all the vessels of the house of God, great and small, and the treasures of the king and of his princes; all these he brought to Babylon.

"And they burned the house of God, and brake down the wall of Jerusalem, and burned all the palaces thereof with fire, and destroyed all the goodly vessels thereof. And them that had escaped from the sword carried he away to Babylon: where they were servants to him and his sons until the reign of the kingdom of Persia."—2 *Chron.* xxxvi. 11–20. * * *

"Now in the first year of Cyrus king of Persia, that

the word of the Lord by the mouth of Jeremiah might be fulfilled, the Lord stirred up the spirit of Cyrus king of Persia, that he made a proclamation throughout all his kingdom, and put it also in writing, saying, Thus saith Cyrus king of Persia, The Lord God of heaven hath given me all the kingdoms of the earth; and he hath charged me to build him a house at Jerusalem, which is in Judah. Who is there among you of all his people? His God be with him, and let him go up to Jerusalem, which is in Judah, and build the house of the Lord God of Israel, which is in Jerusalem."—*Ezra* i. 1–3.

"And Moses said unto God, Behold, when I come unto the children of Israel, and shall say unto them, The God of your fathers hath sent me unto you; and they shall say unto me, What is his name? What shall I say unto them?

"And God said unto Moses, I AM THAT I AM: and he said, Thus shalt thou say unto the children of Israel, I AM hath sent me unto you."—*Exodus* iii. 13, 14. * * * * *

"Lord I cry unto thee: make haste unto me; give ear unto my voice. Let my prayer be set forth before thee as incense, and the lifting up of my hands as the evening sacrifice. Set a watch, O Lord, before my mouth; keep the door of my lips. Incline not my heart to any evil thing, to practice wicked works with men that work iniquity. Let the righteous smite me, it shall be a kindness; let him reprove me, it shall be an excellent oil. Mine eyes are unto thee, O God the Lord; in thee is my trust; leave not my soul destitute. Keep me from the snares which they have laid for me, and the gins of the workers of iniquity. Let the wicked fall into their own nets, whilst that I withal escape."—*Psalm* cxli.

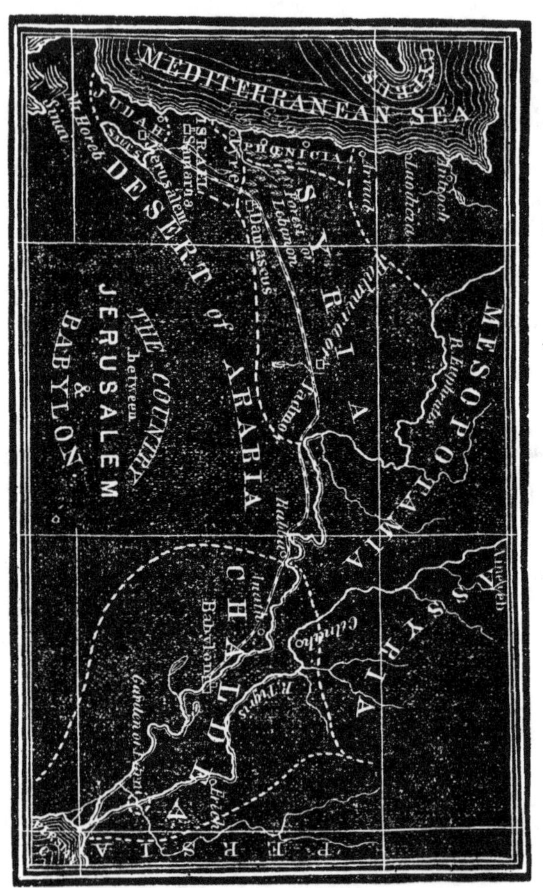
MEDITERRANEAN SEA
JUDAH
ISRAEL
Samaria
Jerusalem
Mt. Horeb
DESERT of ARABIA
PHŒNICIA
SYRIA
Forest of Lebanon
Damascus
Antioch
Laodicea
Palmyra
Tadmor
MESOPOTAMIA
R. Euphrates
THE COUNTRY between JERUSALEM & BABYLON
ASSYRIA
CHALDEA
Babylon
R. Tigris
PERSIA

"I cried unto the Lord with my voice; with my voice unto the Lord did I make my supplication. I poured out my complaint before him: I shewed before him my trouble. When my spirit was overwhelmed within me, then thou knewest my path: in the way wherein I walked, have they privily laid a snare for me. I looked on my right hand, and beheld, but there was no man that would know me: refuge failed me: no man cared for my soul. I cried unto thee, O Lord: I said, Thou art my refuge and my portion in the land of the living. Attend unto my cry; for I am brought very low: deliver me from my persecutors; for they are stronger than I. Bring my soul out of prison, that I may praise thy name."—*Psalm* cxlii. * * * *

"Hear my prayer, O Lord, give ear to my supplications: in thy faithfulness answer me, and in thy righteousness. And enter not into judgment with thy servant: for in thy sight shall no man living be justified. For the enemy hath persecuted my soul; he hath smitten my life down to the ground; he hath made me to dwell in darkness. Therefore is my spirit overwhelmed within me; my heart within me is desolate. Hear me speedily, O Lord: my spirit faileth: hide not thy face from me, lest I be like unto them that go down into the pit. Cause me to hear thy loving kindness in the morning: for in thee do I trust: cause me to know the way wherein I should walk: for I lift my soul unto thee. Teach me to do thy will; for thou art my God: bring my soul out of trouble, and of thy mercy cut off mine enemies, for I am thy servant."—*Psalm* cxliii. * * * * *

"And Moses answered and said, But behold, they will not believe me, nor hearken unto my voice: for they will say, The Lord hath not appeared unto thee. And the Lord said unto him, What is that in thine hand? And he said, A rod. And he said, Cast it on the ground. And he cast it on the ground, and it became a serpent; and Moses fled from before it. And the Lord said unto Moses, Put forth thine hand, and takė it by the tail. And he put forth his hand, and caught it, and it became a rod in his hand. That they may believe that the Lord God of their fathers, the God of Abraham, the God of Isaac, and the God of Jacob, hath appeared unto the. * * * * * *

"And the Lord said furthermore unto him, Put now thine hand into thy bosom. And he put his hand into his bosom: and when he took it out, behold, his hand was leprous as snow. And he said, Put thine hand into thy bosom again. And he put his hand into his bosom again; and plucked it out of his bosom, and, behold, it was turned again as his other flesh. And it shall come to pass, if they will not believe thee, neither hearken unto the voice of the first sign, that they will believe the voice of the latter sign. * * * And it shall come to pass, if they will not believe also these two signs, neither hearken unto thy voice, that thou shalt take the water of the river, and pour it upon the dry land: and the water which thou takest out of the river shall become blood upon the dry land."

Exodus iv. 1–9.

"In the seventh month, in the one and twentieth day of the month, came the word of the Lord by the prophet

Haggai, saying, Speak now to Zerubbabel the son of Shealtiel, governor of Judah, and to Joshua the son of Josedech, the high priest, and to the residue of the people, saying, Who is left among you that saw this house in her first glory? and how do you see it now? Is it not in your eyes in comparison of it as nothing? Yet now be strong, O Zerubbabel, and be strong, O Joshua, son of Josedech, the high priest; and be strong all ye people of the land, and work; for I am with you, according to the word which I covenanted with you when ye came out of Egypt, so my spirit remaineth among you: fear ye not. For thus saith the Lord of Hosts, Yet once, it is a little while, and I will shake the heavens, and the earth, and the sea, and the dry land; and I will shake all nations, and the desire of all nations shall come, and I will fill this house with glory. The silver is mine, and the gold is mine. The glory of this latter house shall be greater than of the former, and in this place will I give peace.

"In that day will I take thee, O Zerubbabel, my servant, the son of Shealtiel, saith the Lord, and will make thee as a signet: for I have chosen thee."

Haggai ii. 1–9, 23.

"This is the word of the Lord unto Zerubbabel, saying, Not by might nor power, but by my spirit. Who art thou, O great mountain? Before Zerubbabel thou shalt become a plain: and he shall bring forth the head stone thereof with shouting, crying, Grace, grace unto it. Moreover, the word of the Lord came unto me saying, The hands of Zerubbabel have laid the foundation of this house; his hands shall also finish it; and thou shalt know that the Lord of Hosts hath sent me unto you. For who hath despised the day of small things? For they shall rejoice, and shall see the plummet in the hand of Zerubbabel, with those seven."—*Zechariah* iv. 6–10.

"In that day will I raise up the tabernacle of David that is fallen, and close up the breaches thereof, and I will raise up his ruin, and I will build it as in the days of old."—*Amos* ix. 11.

"And it came to pass, when Moses had made an end of writing the words of this law in a book, until they were finished, that Moses commanded the Levites which bare the ark of the covenant of the Lord, saying, Take this book of the law, and put it in the side of the ark of the covenant of the Lord your God, that it may be there for a witness against thee."—*Deuteronomy* xxxi. 24–26.

"And thou shalt put the mercy seat above, upon the ark; and in the ark thou shalt put the testimony that I shall give thee."—*Exodus* xxv. 21.

"And Moses said, this is the thing which the Lord commandeth, Fill an omer of the manna, to be kept for your generations; that they may see the bread wherewith I have fed you in the wilderness, when I brought you forth from the land of Egypt. And Moses said

unto Aaron, Take a pot, and put an omer full of manna therein, and lay it up before the Lord, to be kept for your generations. As the Lord commanded Moses, so Aaron laid it up before the testimony to be kept."
Exodus xvi. 32–34.

"And the Lord said unto Moses, Bring Aaron's rod again before the testimony, to be kept for a token."
Numbers xvii. 10.

"For there was a tabernacle made; the first wherein was the candlestick, and the table, and the shew bread; which is called the Sanctuary. And after the veils, the tabernacle, which is called the Holiest of all; which had the golden censer, and the ark of the covenant, overlaid round about with gold, wherein was the golden pot that had manna, and Aaron's rod that budded, and the tables of the covenant; and over it, the cherubims of glory, shadowing the mercy seat; of which we cannot now speak particularly."—*Hebrews* ix. 2–5.

"And God spake unto Moses, and said unto him, I am the Lord: and I appeared unto Abraham, unto Isaac, and unto Jacob, by the name of God Almighty; but by my name JEHOVAH was I not known to them."—*Exodus* vi. 2, 3. * * *

"In the beginning was the Word, and the Word was with God, and the Word was God. The same was in the beginning with God. All things were made by him; and without him was not any thing made that was made. In him was life, and the life was the light of men. And the light shineth in darkness, and the darkness comprehended it not."—*John* i. 1–5.

The following remarks relative to King Solomon's Temple, cannot be uninteresting to a Royal Arch Mason:—

This famous fabric was situated on Mount Moriah, near the place where Abraham was about to offer up his son Isaac, and where David met and appeased the destroying angel, who was visible over the *threshing floor of Ornan the Jebusite.* It was begun in the fourth year of the reign of Solomon; the third after the death of David; four hundred and eighty years after the passage of the Red Sea, and on the second day of the month Zif, being the second month of the sacred year, which answers to the 21st of April, in the year of the world two thousand nine hundred and ninety-two; and was carried on with such prodigious speed, that it was finished, in all its parts, in little more than seven years.

By the masonic art, and the wise regulations of Solomon, this famous edifice was erected without the sound of the axe, hammer, or any tool of iron; for the stones were all hewed, squared and numbered, in the quarries of Zeradatha, where they were raised; the timbers were felled and prepared in the forest of Lebanon, and conveyed by sea in floats to Joppa, and from thence by land to Jerusalem; where the fabric was erected by the assistance of wooden instruments prepared for that purpose. And when the building was finished, its several parts fitted with such exact nicety, that it had more the appearance of being the handywork of the Supreme Architect of the Universe, than of human hands.

In the year of the world 3029, King Solomon died, and was succeeded by his son Rehoboam. Soon after this, instigated and lead on by Jeroboam, the son of Nebat, ten of the tribes revolted against Rehoboam and set up a separate kingdom, with Jeroboam at their head. In this manner were the tribes of Israel divided and under two distinct governments for two hundred and fifty-four years. The ten revolted tribes became weak and degenerated; their country was laid waste, and their government overthrown and extirpated by Salmanezer, King of Assyria. After a series of changes and events, Nebuchadnezzar, King of Babylon, having besieged Jerusalem and raised towers all round the city, so that, after defending it for the space of a year and a half, it was, in the eleventh year of the reign of Zedekiah, King of Judah, surrendered and delivered at midnight to the officers of Nebuchadnezzar, who sacked and destroyed the temple, and took away all the holy vessels, together with those two famous brazen pillars; and the remnant of the people that escaped the sword, carried he away captives to Babylon, where they remained servants to him and his successors until the reign of Cyrus, King of Persia. Cyrus, in the first year of his reign, being directed by that divine power which invisibly led him to the throne of Persia, issued his famous edict for the liberation of the Hebrew captives, with permission that they should return to their native country and rebuild the city and *house of the Lord.* Accordingly, the principal people of the tribes of Judah and Benjamin, with the priests and Levites, immediately departed for Jerusalem and commenced the great and glorious work.

CHARGE TO A NEWLY EXALTED COMPANION.

Worthy Companion—By the consent and assistance of the members of this Chapter, you are now exalted to the sublime and honorable degree of Royal Arch Mason. The rites and mysteries developed in this degree have been handed down through a chosen few, unchanged by time, and uncontrolled by prejudice; and we expect and trust, they will be regarded by you with the same veneration, and transmitted with the same scrupulous purity, to your successors.

No one can reflect on the ceremonies of gaining admission into this place, without being forcibly struck with the important lessons which they teach. Here we are necessarily led to contemplate, with gratitude and admiration, the sacred Source whence all earthly comforts flow. Here we find additional inducements to continue stedfast and immoveable in the discharge of our respective duties; and here we are bound by the most solemn ties, to promote each other's welfare and correct each other's failing by advice, admonition and reproof. As it is our earnest desire, and a duty we owe to our companions of this Order, that the admission of every candidate into this Chapter should be attended by the approbation of the most scrutinizing eye, we hope always to possess the satisfaction of finding none among us but such as will promote, to the utmost of their power, the great end of our institution. By paying due attention to this determination, we expect you will never recommend any candidate to this Chapter, whose abilities and knowledge of the preceding degrees, you cannot freely vouch for, and whom you do not firmly and confidently believe, will fully conform to the principles of our Order, and fulfil the obligations of a Royal Arch Mason. While such are our members, we may expect to be united in one object, without lukewarmness, inattention or neglect; but zeal, fidelity and affection, will be the distinguishing characteristics of our society; and that satisfaction, harmony and peace, may be enjoyed at our meetings, which no other society can afford.

CLOSING PRAYER.

By the *wisdom* of the Supreme High Priest, may we be directed; by his *strength*, may we be enabled; and by the *beauty* of virtue, may we be incited, to perform the obligations here enjoined on us; to keep inviolably the mysteries here unfolded to us; and invariably to practice all those duties out of the Chapter, which are inculcated in it. Amen.

Response. So mote it be.

PART THIRD.

CHAPTER I.

ROYAL MASTER'S DEGREE.

This degree cannot legally be conferred on any but Royal Arch Masons, who have taken all the preceding degrees; and it is preparatory to that of the Select Master. Although it is short, yet it contains some valuable information, and is intimately connected with the degree of Select Master. It also enables us with ease and facility to examine the privileges of others to this degree; while, at the same time, it proves ourselves.

The following passages of Scripture, &c., are considered to be appropriate to this degree:—

"And Solomon made all the vessels that pertained unto the house of the Lord: the altar of gold, and the table of gold, whereupon the shew bread was; and the candlesticks of pure gold; five on the right side, and five on the left, before the oracle; with the flowers and the lamps, and the tongs of gold; and the bowls and the snuffers, and the basons, and the spoons, and the censers, of pure gold; aud the hinges of gold, both for the doors of the inner house, the most holy place, and for the doors of the house, to wit, of the Temple. So

Hiram made an end of doing all the work, that he made for King Solomon, for the house of the Lord."

1 *Kings* vii. 48–50, 40.

"And behold, I come quickly; and my reward is with me, to give every man according as his work shall be. I am Alpha and Omega, the beginning and the end, the first and the last. Blessed are they that do his commandments, that they may have right to the tree of life, and may enter in through the gates into the city."—*Rev.* xxii. 12–14.

"And he set the cherubims within the inner house: and they stretched forth the wings of the cherubims, so that the wing of the one touched the one wall, and the wing of the other cherub touched the other wall, and their wings touched one another in the midst of the house."—1 *Kings* vi. 27.

The Ark, called the glory of Israel, which was seated in the middle of the holy place, under the wings of the cherubim, was a small chest, or coffer, three feet nine inches long, two feet three inches wide, and three feet three inches high. It was made of wood, excepting only the mercy seat, but overlaid with gold, both inside and out. It had a ledge of gold surrounding it at the top, into which the cover, called mercy seat, was let in. The mercy seat was of solid gold, the thickness of a hand's breadth: at the two ends of it were two cherubims, looking inwards towards each other, with their wings expanded; which embracing the whole circumference of the mercy seat, they met on each side, in the middle; all of which, the Rabbins say, was made of the same mass, without any soldering of parts.

Here the Shekinah, or Divine Presence, rested and was visible in the appearance of a cloud over it. From hence the Bathkoll issued, and gave answer when God was consulted. And hence it is that God is said, in the Scripture, to dwell between the cherubim; that is, between the cherubim on the mercy seat, because there was the seat or throne of the visible appearance of his glory among them.

CHAPTER II.

SELECT MASTER'S DEGREE.

This degree is the summit and perfection of ancient masonry; and without which the history of the Royal

Arch Degree cannot be complete. It rationally accounts for the concealment and preservation of the essentials of the Craft which were brought to light at the erection of the second Temple, and which lay concealed from the masonic eye for four hundred and seventy years.

Many particulars relative to those few who, for their superior skill, were selected to complete an important part of King Solomon's Temple, are explained.

And here too is exemplified an instance of *justice* and *mercy*, by our ancient patron, towards one of the Craft, who was lead to disobey his commands, by an over *zealous* attachment for the institution. It ends with a description of a particular circumstance, which characterizes the degree.

The following Psalm is read at opening:

"His foundation is in the holy mountains. The Lord loveth the gates of Zion more than all the dwellings of Jacob. Glorious things are spoken of thee, O city of God. Selah. I will make mention of Rahab and Babylon to them that know me: behold Philistia, and Tyre, with Ethiopia; this man was born there: And of Zion it shall be said, This and that man was born in her; and the Highest himself shall establish her. The Lord shall count, when he writeth up the people, that this man was born there. Selah. As well the singers as the players on instruments shall be there: all my springs are in thee."—*Psalm* lxxxvii.

The following passages of Scripture serve as illustrations here:—

"So King Solomon was king over all Israel. Azariah the son of Nathan was over the officers: and Zabud the son of Nathan was principal officer, and the king's friend; and Ahishar was over the household: and Adoniram the son of Abda was over the tribute."

1 *Kings* iv. 1, 5 and 6.

"And the King commanded, and they brought great stones, costly stones, and hewed stones, to lay the foundation of the house. And Solomon's builders and Hiram's builders did hew them, and the stone-squarers: so they prepared timber and stones to build the house."

1 *Kings* v. 17, 18.

"And King Solomon sent and fetched Hiram out of Tyre. He was a widow's son, of the tribe of Naphtali, and his father was a man of Tyre, a worker of brass; and he was filled with wisdom and understanding, and cunning to work all works in brass."—1 *Kings* vii. 13, 14.

"The ancients of Gebal, and the wise men thereof, were in thee thy calkers: all the ships of the sea, with their mariners, were in thee, to occupy thy merchandize."—*Ezekiel* xxvii. 9.

"And it came to pass, when Moses had made an end of writing the words of this law in a book, until they were finished, that Moses commanded the Levites, which bare the ark of the covenant of the Lord, saying, Take this book of the Law, and put it in the side of the ark of the covenant of the Lord, your God, that it may be there for a witness against thee."—*Deut.* xxxi. 24–26.

"And Moses said unto Aaron, Take a pot, and put an omer full of manna therein, and lay it up before the Lord, to be kept for your generations. As the Lord commanded Moses, so Aaron laid it up before the testimony to be kept."—*Exodus* xvi. 33, 34.

"And the Lord said unto Moses, Bring Aaron's rod again before the testimony, to be kept for a token."

Numbers xvii. 10.

"And when Moses was gone into the tabernacle of the congregation to speak with him, then he heard the voice of one speaking unto him from off the mercy seat that was upon the ark of the testimony, from between the two cherubims: and he spake unto them."

Numbers vii. 89.

"And look that thou make them after their pattern, which was shewed thee in the mount."

Exodus xxv. 40.

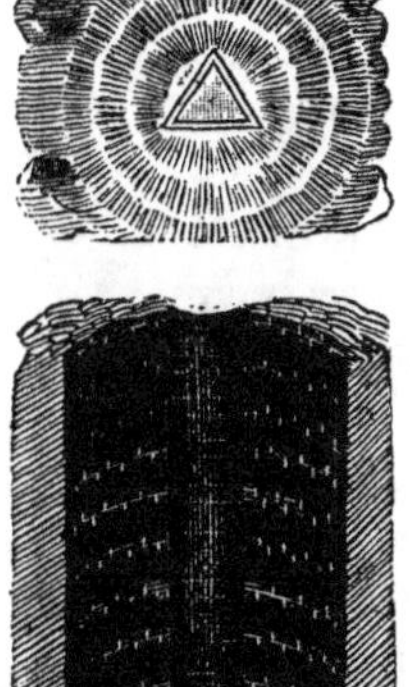

CHARGE TO A SELECT MASTER.

Companion—Having attained to this degree, you have passed the *circle of perfection* in ancient Masonry. In the capacity of Select Master, you must be sensible that your obligations are increased in proportion to your privileges. Let it be your constant care to prove yourself worthy of the confidence reposed in you, in admitting you to this select degree. Let uprightness and integrity attend your steps; let *justice* and *mercy* mark your conduct; let *fervency* and *zeal* stimulate you in the discharge of the various duties incumbent on you; but suffer not an idle or impertinent *curiosity* to lead you astray or betray you into danger. Be *deaf* to every insinuation which would have a tendency to weaken your resolution, or tempt you to an act of *disobedience.* Be voluntarily *dumb* and *blind,* when the exercise of those faculties would endanger the peace of your mind or the probity of your conduct; and let *silence* and *secrecy,* those cardinal virtues of a Select Master, be scrupulously observed on all necessary occasions. By a steady adherence to the important instructions contained in this degree, you will merit the approbation of the select number with whom you are associated, and will enjoy the high satisfaction of having acted well your part in the important enterprise in which you are engaged: and after having *wrought your regular hours,* may you be admitted to participate in all the privileges of a *Select Master.*

PART FOURTH.

CHAPTER I.

ORDER OF HIGH PRIESTHOOD.

THIS order appertains to the office of High Priest of a Royal Arch Chapter; and no one can be legally entitled to receive it, until he has been duly elected to preside as High Priest in a regular Chapter of Royal Arch Masons. This order cannot be conferred unless at least three duly qualified High Priests are present. Whenever the ceremony is performed in due and ample form, the assistance of at least nine High Priests, who have received it, is requisite.

Though the High Priest of every regular Royal Arch Chapter, having himself been duly qualified, can confer the order, under the preceding limitation as to number, yet it is desirable, when circumstances will permit, that it should be conferred by the Grand High Priest of the Grand Royal Arch Chapter, or such Present or Past High Priest as he may designate for that purpose. A convention, notified to meet at the time of any convocation of the Grand Chapter, will afford the best opportunity of conferring this important and exalted degree of masonry with appropriate solemnity. Whenever it is conferred, the following directions are to be observed:—

A candidate desirous of receiving the order of High Priesthood, makes a written request to his predecessor in office, or, when it can be done, to the Grand High Priest, respectfully requesting that a convention of High Priests may be called for the purpose of conferring on him the order. When the convention meets and is duly organized, a certificate of the due election of the candidate to the office of High Priest, must be produced. This certificate is signed by his predecessor in office, attested by the Secretary of the Chapter. On examination of this certificate, the qualifications of the candidate are ascertained. The solemn ceremonies of conferring the order upon him, then ensue. When ended, the presiding officer directs the Secretary of the convention to make a record of the proceedings and return it to the Secretary of the Grand Chapter, to be by him laid before the Grand High Priest for the information of all whom it may concern. The convention of High Priests is then dissolved in due form.

It is the duty of every Companion, as soon after his election to the office of High Priest as is consistent with his personal convenience, to apply for admission to the order of High Priesthood, that he may be fully qualified properly to govern his Chapter.

The following passages of Scripture are made use of during the ceremonies appertaining to this order:

"And they took Lot, Abram's brother's son, who dwelt in Sodom, and his goods, and departed. And there came one that had escaped, and told Abram, the Hebrew; for he dwelt in the plain of Mamre the Amorite, brother of Eschol, and brother of Aner: and these were confederate with Abram.

"And when Abram heard that his brother was taken captive, he armed his trained servants, born in his own house, three hundred and eighteen, and pursued them unto Dan. And he divided himself against them, he and his servants, by night, and smote them, and pursued them unto Hobah, which is on the left hand of Damascus. And he brought back all the goods, and also brought again his brother Lot, and his goods, and the women also, and the people. And the king of Sodom went out to meet him after his return from the slaughter of Chederlaomer, and of the kings that were with him, at the valley of Shaveh, which is the king's dale.

"And Melchisedek, king of Salem, brought forth bread and wine: and he was the priest of the Most High God. And he blessed him, and said, Blessed be Abram of the Most High God, who hath delivered thine enemies into thy hand. And he gave him tithes of all. And the king of Sodom said to Abram, Give me the persons, and take the goods to thyself. And Abram said to the king of Sodom, I have lifted up mine hand to the Lord, the Most High God, the possessor of heaven and earth, that I will not take from a thread even to a shoe-latchet, and that I will not take any thing that is thine, lest thou shouldest say, I have made Abram rich: save only that which the young men have

eaten, and the portion of the men which went with me, Aner, Eschol, and Mamre; let them take their portion."
Genesis xiv. 12–24.

"For this Melchisedek, king of Salem, priest of the Most High God, who met Abraham returning from the slaughter of the kings, and blessed him: to whom also Abraham gave a tenth part of all: first being by interpretation King of Righteousness, and after that also King of Salem, which is, King of Peace; without father, without mother, without descent, having neither beginning of days nor end of life; but made like unto the Son of God; abideth a priest continually. Now consider how great this man was, unto whom even the patriarch Abraham gave the tenth of the spoils. And verily, they that are the sons of Levi, who receive the office of priesthood, have a commandment to take tithes of the people, according to the law, that is, of their brethren, though they come out of the loins of Abraham.

"For he testifieth, Thou art a priest for ever after the order of Melchisedek.

"And inasmuch as not without an oath he was made priest: (for those priests [under the Levitical law] were made without an oath; but this with an oath by him that said unto him, The Lord sware and will not repent, Thou art a priest for ever, after the order of Melchisedek.)"—*Heb.* vii. 1–6, 17, 20–1.

"And the Lord spake unto Moses, saying, speak unto Aaron, and unto his sons, saying, On this wise ye shall bless the children of Israel, saying unto them, The Lord bless thee, and keep thee; the Lord make his face to shine upon thee and be gracious unto thee; the Lord lift up his countenance upon thee and give thee peace."

CHAPTER II.

CEREMONY AND CHARGE UPON THE INSTALLATION OF THE OFFICERS OF A ROYAL ARCH CHAPTER.

1. The Grand Officers will meet at a convenient place, and open.

2. The subordinate Chapter will meet in the outer courts of their Hall, and form an avenue for the reception of the Grand Officers.

3. When formed, they will despatch a committee to the place where the Grand Officers are assembled to inform the Grand Marshal that the Chapter is prepared to receive them;—the Grand Marshal will announce the committee, and introduce them to the Grand Officers.

4. The Grand Officers will move in procession, conducted by the committee, to the Hall of the Chapter, in the following order:

Grand Tyler,
Two Grand Stewards:
Representatives of Subordinate Chapters, according to seniority, by threes triangular;
Three Great Lights;
Orator, Chaplain, and other clergy;
Grand Secretary, Grand Treasurer, and Grand Royal Arch Captain;
Grand P. Sojourner, Grand Captain of the Host, and Deputy Grand High Priest;

Grand Scribe, Grand King, and Grand High Priest;
(Grand Marshal, on the left of the procession.)

N. B. The Grand Captain of the Host, Grand Principal Sojourner, and Grand Royal Arch Captain, are appointed pro tempore.

When the Grand High Priest enters, the Grand Honors are given.

5. The Grand Secretary will then call over the names of the officers elect; and the Grand High Priest will ask whether they accept their respective offices. If they answer in the affirmative, he then asks the members whether they remain satisfied with their choice. If they answer in the affirmative, he directs their officers to approach the sacred volume, and become qualified for Installation, agreeably to the 4th section of the 4th article of the General Grand Royal Arch Constitution.

6. The Grand Marshal will then form the whole in procession, and they will march through the *veils* into the inner apartment, where they will surround the altar, which is previously prepared in *ample form* for the occasion.

7. All present will kneel, and the following prayer will be recited:

PRAYER.

Almighty and Supreme High Priest of heaven and earth! Who is there in heaven but thee! and who upon earth can stand in competition with thee! Thy

OMNISCIENT MIND brings all things in review, past, present, and to come; thine OMNIPOTENT ARM directs the movements of the vast creation; thine OMNIPRESENT EYE pervades the secret recesses of every heart; thy boundless beneficence supplies us with every comfort and enjoyment; and thine unspeakable perfections and glory surpass the understanding of the children of men! Our Father, who art in heaven, we invoke thy benediction upon the purposes of our present assembly. Let this Chapter be established to thine honor: let its officers be endowed with wisdom to discern, and fidelity to pursue, its true interests; let its members be ever mindful of the duty they owe to their God, the obedience they owe to their superiors, the love they owe to their equals, and the good will they owe to all mankind. Let this Chapter be consecrated to thy glory, and its members ever exemplify their love to God by their beneficence to man.

"Glory be to God on high." Amen.

Response, "So mote it be."

They are then qualified in due form.

All the Companions, except High Priests and Past High Priests, are then desired to withdraw, while the new High Priest is solemnly bound to the performance of his duties; and after the performance of other necessary ceremonies, not proper to be written, they are permitted to return.

8. The whole then repair to their appropriate stations, when the Grand Marshal will form a general procession in the following order:

Captain of the Host;

Three Royal Arch Stewards, with rods;
Tyler of a Blue Lodge;
Entered Apprentices;
Fellow Crafts;
Master Masons;
Stewards of Lodges, having Jewels;
Deacons, having Jewels;
Secretaries, having Jewels;
Treasurers, having Jewels;
Wardens, having Jewels;
Mark Master Masons;
Most Excellent Masters;
Royal Arch Masons, by three;
Royal Masters, by three,
Select Masters, by three;
Orders of Knighthood;
Tyler of the new Chapter;
Members of the new Chapter, by three;
Three Masters of Veils;
Secretary, Treasurer, Royal Arch Captain, and
Principal Sojourner carrying the Ark;
A Companion, carrying the Pot of Incense;
Two Companions carrying Lights;
Scribe, High Priest, and King;
Grand Chapter, as before prescribed.

On arriving at the church or house where the services

are to be performed, they halt, open to the right and left, and face inward, while the Grand Officers and others in succession pass through and enter the house.

9. The officers and members of the new Chapter, and also of the Grand Chapter, being seated, the Grand Marshal proclaims silence, and the ceremonies commence.

10. An Anthem or Ode is to be performed.

11. An Oration or Address is to be delivered.

12. An Ode or piece of Music.

*[13. The Deputy Grand High Priest then rises and informs the Grand High Priest, that "a number of Companions, duly instructed in the sublime mysteries, being desirous of promoting the honor, and propagating the principles of the Art, have applied to the Grand Chapter for a warrant to constitute a new Chapter of Royal Arch Masons, which having been obtained, they are now assembled for the purpose of being constituted, and having their officers installed in due and ancient form."]

[14. The Grand Marshal will then form the officers and members of the new Chapter in front of the Grand Officers; after which, the Grand High Priest directs the Grand Secretary to read the Warrant.]

---

* Note. Those paragraphs which are inclosed within brackets, apply exclusively to cases when new Chapters are constituted, and their officers installed for the first time. The rest apply equally to such cases, as well as to annual Installations.

[15. The Grand High Priest then rises and says, "By virtue of the high powers in me vested, I do form you, my respected Companions, into a regular Chapter of Royal Arch Masons. From henceforth you are authorized and empowered to open and hold a Lodge of Mark Masters, Past Masters, and Most Excellent Masters, and a Chapter of Royal Arch Masons; and to do and perform all such things as thereunto may appertain: conforming, in all your doings, to the General Grand Royal Arch Constitution, and the general regulations of the State Grand Chapter. And may the God of your fathers be with you, guide and direct you in all your doings."]

16. The furniture, clothing, jewels, implements, utensils, &c., belonging to the Chapter, (having been previously placed in the center, in front of the Grand Officers, covered,) are now uncovered and the new Chapter is dedicated in due and ancient form.

17. The dedication then follows, the Grand Chaplain saying,

"To our Most Excellent Patron ZERUBBABEL, we solemnly dedicate this Chapter. May the blessing of our Heavenly High Priest descend and rest upon its members, and may their felicity be immortal.

"Glory be to God on high."

[Response by the Companions.]

"As it was in the beginning, is now, and ever shall be; world without end. Amen. So mote it be."

18. The Grand Marshal then says, "I am directed to proclaim, and I do hereby proclaim this Chapter, by the name of ——— Chapter, duly consecrated, constituted and dedicated. This," &c. &c. date.

19. An Ode.

20. The Deputy Grand High Priest will then present the first officer of the new Chapter to the Grand High Priest, saying,

Most Excellent Grand High Priest:—I present you my worthy Companion —— ———, nominated in the warrant, to be installed High Priest of this [new] Chapter. I find him to be skilful in the royal art, and attentive to the moral precepts of our forefathers, and have therefore no doubt but he will discharge the duties of his office with fidelity.

The Grand High Priest then addresses him as follows:

Most Excllent—I feel much satisfaction in performing my duty on the present occasion, by installing you into the office of High Priest of this [new] Chapter. It is an office highly honorable to all those who diligently perform the important duties annexed to it. Your reputed masonic knowledge, however, precludes the necessity of a particular enumeration of those duties. I shall therefore only observe, that by a frequent recurrence to the Constitution and General Regulations, and constant practice of the several sublime lectures and charges, you will be best able to fulfil them; and

I am confident that the Companions who are chosen to preside with you, will give strength to your endeavors, and support to your exertions.

I shall now propose certain questions to you, relative to the duties of your office, and to which I must request your unequivocal answer.

1. Do you solemnly promise that you will use your endeavors to correct the vices, purify the morals, and promote the happiness of those of your Companions who have attained this sublime degree?

2. That you will never suffer your Chapter to be opened, unless there be present nine regular Royal Arch Masons?

3. That you will never suffer either more or less than three brethren to be exalted in your Chapter at one and the same time?

4. That you will not exalt any one to this degree who has not shown a charitable and humane disposition; or who has not made a considerable proficiency in the foregoing degrees?

5. That you will promote the general good of our Order, and, on all proper occasions, be ready to give and receive instructions, and particularly from the General and State Grand Officers?

6. That, to the utmost of your power, you will preserve the solemnities of our ceremonies, and behave, in open Chapter, with the most profound respect and reverence, as an example to your Companions?

7. That you will not acknowledge or have intercourse

with any Chapter that does not work under a constitutional warrant or dispensation?

8. That you will not admit any visiter into your Chapter, who has not been exalted in a Chapter legally constituted, without his being first formally healed?

9. That you will observe and support such by-laws as may be made by your Chapter, in conformity to the General Grand Royal Arch Constitution, and the General Regulations of the Grand Chapter?

10. That you will pay respect and due obedience to the instructions of the General and State Grand Officers, particularly relating to the several Lectures and Charges, and will resign the chair to them, severally, when they may visit your Chapter?

11. That you will support and observe the General Grand Royal Arch Constitution, and the General Regulations of the Grand Royal Arch Chapter, under whose authority you act?

Do you submit to all these things, and do you promise to observe and practice them faithfully?

These questions being answered in the affirmative, the Companions all kneel in due form, and the Grand High Priest or Grand Chaplain repeats the following, or some other suitable prayer:

"Most holy and glorious Lord God, the Great High Priest of Heaven and Earth:—

"We approach thee with reverence and implore thy blessing on the Companion appointed to preside over this new assembly, and now prostrate before thee; fill his heart with thy fear, that his tongue and actions may promote thy glory. Make him steadfast in thy service; grant him firmness of mind; animate his heart, and strengthen his endeavors; may he teach thy judgments and thy laws; and may the incense he shall put before thee, upon thine altar, prove an acceptable sacrifice unto thee. Bless him, O Lord, and bless the work of his hands. Accept us in mercy; hear thou from Heaven thy dwelling-place, and forgive our transgressions.

"Glory be to God the Father; as it was in the beginning," &c.

Response. "So mote it be."

21. The Grand High Priest will then cause the High Priest elect to be invested with his clothing, badges, &c.; after which he will address him as follows, viz:

MOST EXCELLENT—In consequence of your cheerful acquiescence with the charges which you have heard recited, you are qualified for installation as the High Priest of this Royal Arch Chapter; and it is incumbent upon me, on this occasion, to point out some of the particulars appertaining to your office, duty and dignity.

All legally constituted bodies of Royal Arch Masons, are called Chapters; as regular bodies of Masons of the preceding degrees are called Lodges. Every Chapter ought to assemble for work at least once in three months; and must consist of a High Priest, King, Scribe, Captain of the Host, Principal Sojourner, Royal Arch Captain, three Grand Masters of the Veils, Treasurer, Secretary, and as many members as may be found convenient for working to advantage.

The officers of the Chapter officiate in the Lodges, holden for conferring the preparatory degrees, according to rank, as follows, viz:

The High Priest, as Master;
The King, as Senior Warden;
The Scribe, as Junior Warden;
The Captain of the Host, as Marshal or Master of Ceremonies;
The Principal Sojourner, as Senior Deacon;
The Royal Arch Captain, as Junior Deacon;
The Master of the first Veil, as Junior Overseer;
The Master of the second Veil, as Senior Overseer;
The Master of the third Veil, as Master Overseer;
The Treasurer, Secretary, Chaplain, Stewards, and Tyler, as officers of corresponding rank.

The High Priest of every Chapter has it in special charge, to see that the by-laws of his Chapter, as well as the General Grand Royal Arch Constitution, and all the regulations of the Grand Chapter, are duly observed:—that all the officers of his Chapter perform the duties of their respective offices faithfully, and are examples of diligence and industry to their Companions; that true and accurate records of all the proceedings of the Chapter are kept by the Secretary;—that the Treasurer keep and render exact and just accounts of all the moneys and other property belonging to the Chapter; that the regular returns be made annually to the Grand Chapter; and that the annual dues to the Grand Chapter be regularly and punctually paid. He has the right and authority of calling his Chapter together at pleasure, upon any emergency or occurrence, which in his judgment may require their meeting. It is his privilege and duty, together with the King and Scribe, to attend the meetings of the Grand Chapter, either in person or by proxy; and the well-being of the institution requires that this duty on no occasion be omitted.

The office of High Priest is a station highly honorable to those who diligently perform the important duties annexed to it. By a frequent recurrence to the Constitution and General Regulations, and a constant practice of the several sublime Lectures and Charges, you will be best enabled to fulfil those duties; and I am confident that the Companions who are chosen to preside with you, will give strength to your endeavors, and support to your exertions.

Let the *Mitre*, with which you are invested, remind you of the dignity of the office you sustain, and its inscription impress upon your mind a sense of your dependence upon God; that perfection is not given unto man upon earth, and that perfect holiness belongeth alone unto the Lord.

The *Breast-plate,* with which you are decorated, in imitation of that upon which were engraven the names of the twelve tribes, and worn by the High Priests of Israel, is to teach you that you are always to bear in mind your responsibility to the laws and ordinances of the institution, and that the honor and interests of your Chapter and its members should be always near your heart.

The *various colors* of the *Robes* you wear, are emblematical of every grace and virtue which can adorn and beautify the human mind; each of which will be briefly illustrated in the course of the charges to be delivered to your subordinate officers.

You will now take charge of your officers, standing upon their right, and present them severally in succession to the Deputy Grand High Priest, by whom they will be presented to me for installation.

22. The High Priest of the Chapter will then present his second officer to the Deputy Grand High Priest, who will present him to the Grand High Priest in the words of the Constitution. The Grand High Priest will then ask him whether he has attended to the ancient charges and regulations before recited to his superior officcr: if he answers in the affirmative, he is asked whether he fully and freely assents to the same: if he answers in the affirmative, the Grand High Priest

directs his Deputy to invest him with the clothing, &c., and then addresses him as follows, viz:

CHARGE TO THE SECOND OFFICER, OR KING.

Excellent Companion—The important station to which you are elected in this Chapter, requires from you exemplary conduct; its duties demand your most assiduous attention; you are to second and support your chief in all the requirements of his office; and should casualties at any time prevent his attendance, you are to succeed him in the performance of his duties.

Your badge (*the Level surmounted by a crown,*) should remind you, that although you are the representative of a king, and exalted by office above your Companions, yet that you remain upon a level with them, as respects your duty to God, to your neighbor and to yourself; that you are equally bound with them to be obedient to the laws and ordinances of the Institution, to be charitable, humane and just, and to seek every occasion of doing good.

Your office teaches a striking lesson of humility. The institutions of political society teach us to consider the king as the chief of created beings, and that the first duty of his subjects is to obey his mandates; but the institutions of our sublime degrees, by placing the King in a situation subordinate to the High Priest, teaches us that our duty to God is paramount to all other duties, and should ever claim the priority of our obedience to man; and that however strongly we may

12

be bound to obey the laws of civil society, yet that those laws, to be just, should never intermeddle with matters of conscience, nor dictate articles of faith.

The *Scarlet Robe,* an emblem of imperial dignity, should remind you of the paternal concern you should ever feel for the welfare of your Chapter, and the *fervency* and *zeal* with which you should endeavor to promote its prosperity.

In presenting to you the Crown, which is an emblem of royalty, I would remind you, that to reign sovereign in the hearts and affections of men, must be far more grateful to a generous and benevolent mind, than to rule over their lives and fortunes; and that to enable you to enjoy this pre-eminence with honor and satisfaction, you must subject your own passions and prejudices to the dominion of reason and charity.

You are entitled to the second seat in the council of your Companions. Let the bright example of your illustrious predecessor in the Grand Council at Jerusalem, stimulate you to the faithful discharge of your duties; and when the King of kings shall summon you into his immediate presence, from his hand may you receive a *crown of glory,* which shall never fade away.

23. The king will then retire to the line of officers, and the Scribe will be presented in the manner before mentioned. After his investiture, the Grand High Priest will address him as follows, viz:

CHARGE TO THE THIRD OFFICER, OR SCRIBE.

Excellent Companion—The office of Scribe, to which you are elected, is very important and respectable. In the absence of your superior officers, you are bound to succeed them, and to perform their duties The purposes of the institution ought never to suffer for want of intelligence in its proper officers; you will therefore perceive the necessity there is of your possessing such qualifications as will enable you to accomplish those duties which are incumbent upon you, in your appropriate station, as well as those which may occasionally devolve on you, by the absence of your superiors.

The *Purple Robe,* with which you are invested, is an emblem of *union,* and is calculated to remind you that the harmony and unanimity of the Chapter should be your constant aim; and to this end you are studiously to avoid all occasions of giving offence, or countenancing any thing that may create divisions or dissentions. You are, by all means in your power, to endeavor to establish a permanent union and good understanding among all orders and degrees of masonry; and, as the glorious sun, at its meridian height, dispels the mist and clouds which obscure the horizon, so may your exertions tend to dissipate the gloom of jealousy and discord, whenever they may appear.

Your badge (*a Plumb-rule surmounted by the Turban,*) is an emblem of rectitude and vigilance; and while you stand as a watchman upon the tower, to guard your Companions against the approach of those enemies of human felicity, *intemperance* and *excess*, let this faithful monitor ever remind you to walk uprightly in your station; admonishing and animating your Companions to fidelity and industry while at labor, and to temperance and moderation while at refreshment. And when the Great Watchman of Israel, whose eye never slumbers nor sleeps, shall relieve you from your post on earth, may he permit you in heaven to participate in that food and refreshment which is

> "Such as the saints in glory love
> And such as angels eat."

24. The Scribe will then retire to the line of officers, and the next officer be presented as before.

CHARGE TO THE FOURTH OFFICER, OR CAPTAIN OF THE HOST.

Companion—The office with which you are entrusted is of high importance, and demands your most zealous consideration. The preservation of the most essential traits of our ancient customs, usages and landmarks, are within your province; and it is indispensably necessary, that the part assigned to you, in the immediate practice of our rites and ceremonies should be perfectly understood and correctly administered.

Your office corresponds with that of Marshal, or Master of Ceremonies. You are to superintend all processions of your Chapter, when moving as a distinct body, either in public or private; and as the world can only judge of our private discipline by our public deportment, you will be careful that the utmost order and decorum be observed on all such occasions. You will ever be attentive to the commands of your chief, and always near at hand to see them duly executed. I invest you with the badge of your office, and presume that you will give to your duties all that study and attention which their importance demands.

25. He will then retire to the line of officers, and the next officer will be presented.

CHARGE TO THE FIFTH OFFICER, OR PRINCIPAL SOJOURNER.

Companion—The office confided to you, though subordinate in degree, is equal in importance to any in the Chapter, that of your chief alone excepted. Your office corresponds with that of *senior deacon* in the preparatory degrees. Among the duties required of you, the preparation and introduction of candidates are not the least. As in our intercourse with the world experience teaches that first impressions are often the most durable and the most difficult to eradicate, so it is of great importance in all cases, that those impressions should be correct and just: hence it is essential that the officer, who brings the blind by a way that they knew not, and leads them in paths that they have not known, should always be well qualified to make darkness light before them, and crooked things straight.

Your *robe of office* is an emblem of humility, and teaches that in the prosecution of a laudable undertaking we should never decline taking any part that may be assigned us, although it may be the most difficult or dangerous.

The *rose-colored tessellated Border*, adorning your robe, is an emblem of ardor and perseverance, and signifies that when we have engaged in a virtuous course, notwithstanding all the impediments, hardships and trials we may be destined to encounter, we should endure them all with fortitude, and ardently persevere unto the end; resting assured of receiving, at the termination of our labors, a noble and glorious reward. Your past exertions will be considered as a pledge of your future assiduity in the faithful discharge of your duties.

26. He will then retire to the line of officers, and the next officer is presented.

CHARGE TO THE SIXTH OFFICER, OR ROYAL ARCH CAPTAIN.

Companion—The well-known duties of your station require but little elucidation. Your office in the preparatory degrees corresponds with that of *junior deacon*. It is your province, conjointly with the Captain of the Host, to attend the examination of all visiters, and to take care that none are permitted to enter the Chapter but such as have *travelled the rugged path* of trial, and evinced their title to our favor and friendship. You will be attentive to obey the commands of the Captain of the Host, during the *introduction of strangers among* the workmen: and should they be permitted to pass your post, they may by him be introduced into the presence of the Grand Council.

The *White Banner* entrusted to your care, is emblematical of that purity of heart and rectitude of conduct which ought to actuate all those who pass the white veil of the sanctuary. I give it to you strictly in charge, never to suffer any one to pass your post without the *signet of truth.*

I present you the badge of your office, in expectation of your performing your duties with intelligence, assiduity, and propriety

27. He then retires, and the Three Grand Masters of the Veils are presented together.

CHARGE TO THE MASTER OF THE THIRD VEIL.

Companion—I present you with the *Scarlet Banner,* which is the ensign of your office, and with a sword to protect and defend the same. The rich and beautiful color of your banner is emblematical of *fervency* and *zeal;* it is the appropriate color of the Royal Arch degree: it admonishes us, that we should be fervent in the exercise of our devotions to God; and zealous in our endeavors to promote the happiness of man.

CHARGE TO THE MASTER OF THE SECOND VEIL.

Companion—I invest you with the *Purple Banner*, which is the ensign of your office, and arm you with a sword to enable you to maintain its honor.

The color of your banner is produced by a due mixture of *blue* and *scarlet;* the former of which is the characteristic color of the *symbolic* or *first three degrees of masonry*, and the latter, that of the *royal arch degree*. It is an emblem of *union*, and is the characteristic color of the intermediate degrees. It admonishes us to cultivate and improve that spirit of union and harmony between the brethren of the symbolic degrees which should ever distinguish the members of a society founded upon the principles of everlasting truth and universal philanthropy.

CHARGE TO THE MASTER OF THE FIRST VEIL.

Companion—I invest you with the *Blue Banner*, which is the ensign of your office, and a sword for its defence and protection. The color of your banner is one of the most durable and beautiful in nature. It is the appropriate color adopted and worn by our ancient brethren of the three symbolic degrees, and is the peculiar characteristic of an institution which has stood the test of ages, and which is as much distinguished by the durability of its materials or principles, as by the beauty of its superstructure. It is an emblem of universal friendship and benevolence; and instructs us, that in the mind of a Mason those virtues should be as expansive as the blue arch of heaven itself.

CHARGE TO THE THREE MASTERS OF THE VEILS, AS OVERSEERS.

Companions—Those who are placed as overseers of any work, should be well qualified to judge of its beauties and deformities, its excellencies and defects; they should be capable of estimating the former, and amending the latter. This consideration should induce you to cultivate and improve all those qualifications with which you are already endowed, as well as to persevere in your endeavors to acquire those in which you are deficient. Let the various *colors* and *banners* committed to your charge, admonish you to the exercise of the several virtues of which they are emblematic: and you are to enjoin the practice of those virtues upon all who shall present themselves, or the *work* of their hands, *for your inspection.* Let no work receive your approbation but such as is calculated to adorn and strengthen the masonic edifice. Be industrious and faithful in practising and disseminating a knowledge of the *true and perfect work* which alone can stand the test of the *Grand Overseer's Square,* in the great day of trial and retribution. Then, although every *rod* should become a *serpent,* and every serpent an enemy to this institution, yet shall their utmost exertions to destroy its reputation, or sap its foundation, become as impotent as the *leprous hand,* or as *water spilled upon the ground,* which cannot be gathered up again.

28. They then retire, and the Treasurer is presented.

CHARGE TO THE TREASURER.

COMPANION—You are elected Treasurer of this Chapter, and I have the pleasure of investing you with the badge of your office. The qualities which should recommend a Treasurer, are *accuracy* and *fidelity;* accuracy, in keeping a fair and minute account of all receipts and disbursements; fidelity, in carefully preserving all the property and funds of the Chapter that may be placed in his hands, and rendering a just account of the same, whenever he is called upon for that purpose. I presume that your respect for the institution, your attachment to the interests of your Chapter, and your regard for a good name, which is better than precious ointment, will prompt you to the faithful discharge of the duties of your office.

29. He then retires, and the Secretary is presented.

CHARGE TO THE SECRETARY.

COMPANION—I with pleasure invest you with your badge as Secretary of this Chapter. The qualities which should recommend a Secretary, are *promptitude* in issuing the notifications and orders of his superior officers; *punctuality* in attending the convocations of the Chapter; *correctness* in recording their proceedings;

judgment in discriminating between what is proper and what is improper to be committed to writing; *regularity* in making his annual returns to the Grand Chapter; *integrity* in accounting for all moneys that may pass through his hands; and *fidelity* in paying the same over into the hands of the Treasurer. The possession of these good qualities, I presume, has designated you as a suitable candidate for this important office; and I cannot entertain a doubt that you will discharge its duties beneficially to the Chapter, and honorably to yourself. And when you shall have completed the record of your transactions here below, and finished the term of your probation, may you be admitted into the celestial Grand Chapter of saints and angels, and find your name recorded in the book of life eternal.

30. He then retires, and the Chaplain is presented.

CHARGE TO THE CHAPLAIN.

E. AND REV'D. COMPANION—You are appointed Chaplain of this Chapter; and I now invest you with this circular Jewel, the badge of your office. It is emblematical of eternity, and reminds us that here is not our abiding place. Your inclination will undoubtedly conspire with your duty, when you perform in the Chapter those solemn services which created beings should constantly render to their infinite Creator; and which, when offered by one whose holy profession it is, "to point to heaven and lead the way," may, by refining our morals, strengthening our virtues, and purifying our minds, prepare us for admission into the society of those above, whose happiness will be as endless as it is perfect.

31. He then retires, and the Stewards are presented.

CHARGE TO THE STEWARDS.

Companions—You are elected Stewards of this Chapter, I with pleasure invest you with the badges of your office. It is your province to see that every necessary preparation is made for the convenience and accommodation of the Chapter, previous to the time appointed for meeting. You are to see that the clothing, implements and furniture of each degree respectively are properly disposed, and in suitable array for use, whenever they may be required, and that they are secured and proper care taken of them, when the business of the Chapter is over. You are to see that necessary refreshments are provided, and that all your companions, and particularly visiters, are suitably accommodated and supplied. You are to be frugal and prudent in your disbursements, and to be careful that no extravagance or waste is committed in your department; and when you have faithfully fulfilled your stewardship here below, may you receive from heaven the happy greeting of "Well done, good and faithful servant."

32. They then retire, and the Tyler is presented.

CHARGE TO THE TYLER.

Companion—You are appointed Tyler of this Chapter, and I invest you with the badge, and this implement of your office. As the sword is placed in the hands of the Tyler, to enable him effectually to guard against the approach of *cowans and eves-droppers,* and suffer none to pass or repass but such as are *duly qualified;* so it should morally serve as a constant admonition to us to set a guard at the entrance of our thoughts; to place a watch at the door of our lips; and to post a sentinel at the avenue of our actions; thereby excluding every unqualified and unworthy thought, word and deed; and preserving consciences void of offence towards God and towards man.

As the first application from visiters for admission into the Chapter is generally made to the Tyler at the door, your station will often present you to the observation of strangers; it is therefore essentially necessary that he who sustains the office with which you are entrusted should be a man of good morals, steady habits, strict discipline, temperate, affable, and discreet. I trust that a regard for the honor and reputation of the institution will ever induce you to perform with fidelity the trust reposed in you; and when the door of this earthly tabernacle shall be closed, may you find an abundant entrance through the gates into the temple and city of our God.

33. He will then retire, and then follows an

ADDRESS TO THE HIGH PRIEST.

M. E. Companion—Having been honored with the free suffrage of the members of this Chapter, you are elected to the most important office which it is within their power to bestow. This expression of their esteem and respect should draw from you corresponding sensations; and your demeanor should be such as to repay the honor they have so conspicuously conferred upon you, by an honorable and faithful discharge of the duties of your office. The station you are called to fill is important, not only as it respects the correct practice of our rites and ceremonies, and the internal economy of the Chapter over which you preside, but the public reputation of the institution will be generally found to rise or fall according to the skill, fidelity and descretion with which its concerns are managed, and in proportion as the character and conduct of its principal officers are estimable or censurable.

You have accepted a trust to which is attached a weight of responsibility that will require all your efforts to discharge honorably to yourself, and satisfactorily to the Chapter. You are to see that your officers are capable and faithful in the exercise of their offices. Sould they lack ability, you are expected to supply their defects; you are to watch carefully the progress of their performances, and to see that the long established customs of the institution suffer no derangement in their hands. You are to have a careful eye over the general conduct of the Chapter; see that due order and subordination is observed on all occasions; that the members are properly instructed; that due solemnity be observed in the practice of our rites; that no improper levity be permitted at any time, but more especially at the introduction of strangers among the workmen.

In fine, you are to be an example to your officers and members, which they need not hesitate to follow; thus securing to yourself the favor of Heaven, and the applause of your brethren and companions.

ADDRESS TO THE OFFICERS GENERALLY.

Companions in office—Precept and example should ever advance with equal pace. Those moral duties which you are required to teach unto others, you should never neglect to practice yourselves.

Do you desire that the demeanor of your equals and inferiors towards you, should be marked with deference and respect? Be sure that you omit no opportunity of furnishing them with examples in your own conduct towards your superiors. Do you desire to obtain instruction from those who are more wise or better informed than yourself? Be sure that you are always ready to impart of your knowledge to those within your sphere, who stand in need of, and are entitled to receive it. Do you desire distinction among your companions? Be sure that your claims to preferment are founded upon superior attainments; let no ambitious passion be suffered to induce you to envy or supplant a companion who may be considered as better qualified for promotion than yourselves; but rather let a laudable emulation induce you to strive to excel each other in improvement and discipline; ever remembering, that he who faithfully performs his duty, even in a subordinate or private station, is as justly entitled to esteem and respect, as he who is invested with supreme authority.

ADDRESS TO THE CHAPTER AT LARGE.

Companions—The exercise and management of the sublime degrees of masonry in your Chapter hitherto, are so highly appreciated, and the good reputation of the Chapter so well established, that I must presume these considerations alone, were there no others of greater magnitude, would be sufficient to induce you to preserve and perpetuate this valuable and honorable character. But when to these is added the pleasure which every philanthropic heart must feel in doing good, in promoting good order, in diffusing light and knowledge, in cultivating masonic and Christian charity, which are the great objects of this sublime institution, I cannot doubt that your future conduct, and that of your successors, will be calculated still to increase the lustre of your justly esteemed reputation.

May your *Chapter* become *beautiful* as the *Temple*, *peaceful* as the *Ark*, and *sacred* as its *most holy place*. May your oblations of *piety* and *praise* be *grateful* as the *incense;* your love *warm* as its *flame*, and your *charity* diffusive as its *fragrance*. May your hearts be *pure* as the *altar*, and your conduct *acceptable* as the *offering*.

May the exercise of your *charity* be as constant as the returning wants of the distressed *widow* and helpless *orphan*. May the approbation of Heaven be your encouragement, and the testimony of a good conscience be your support. May you be endowed with every good and perfect gift, while *travelling* the *rugged path* of life, and finally be *admitted within the veil* of heaven, to the full enjoyment of life eternal.

Amen. So mote it be.

34. The officers and members of the Chapter will then pass in review in front of the Grand Officers, with their hands crossed on their breasts, bowing as they pass.

35. The Grand Marshal will then proclaim the Chapter, by the name of ———, to be regularly constituted, and its officers duly installed.

36. The ceremonies conclude with an Ode, or appropriate piece of music.

37. The procession is then formed, when they return to the place whence they set out.

38. When the Grand Officers retire, the Chapter will form an avenue for them to pass through, and salute them with the grand honors. The two bodies then separately close their respective Chapters.

MASONIC FUNERAL SERVICE,

AS ADOPTED BY THE

GRAND LODGE OF OHIO.

[We have concluded to add the following Funeral Service, adopted by the Grand Lodge of Ohio: and Brethren may elect which to use, this, or that included in the degree of Past Master.]

GENERAL DIRECTIONS.

I. No brother can be interred with the formalities of the Order unless he has received the *Third Degree* in masonry.

II. The Master of a Lodge being notified of the death of a brother, and of his request to be buried with masonic ceremonies, shall convene his Lodge and make all suitable arrangements to that effect.

III. If two or more Lodges attend, the ceremonies will be conducted by the Lodge of which the deceased was a member. In the case of a *Stranger* or *Sojourner*, the Master of the Senior Lodge present will preside.

IV. All the brethren who walk in procession should observe as much as possible an uniformity of dress. A proper badge of mourning around the left arm, with white gloves and aprons, are most suitable. It is recommended to avoid all ostentatious display of masonic costume.

V. Musicians, if belonging to the Fraternity, will walk in procession immediately after the Tyler; if they are not Masons, they will precede him. Solemn and appropriate pieces of music only should be performed; all others are especially interdicted.

VI. The cushion on which the Holy Bible is placed, should be covered with black; a piece of black crape should be tied around all the furniture carried in procession, around each Steward's rod, and on the musical instruments. The procession will immediately precede the corpse, and the brethren walk two and two, except such officers as from their station are to walk otherwise.

VII. It would be proper for each Lodge, when convenient, to have a pall of black cloth, velvet, or other suitable material, to be used on funeral occasions. On the coffin will be placed or tied a white apron.

VIII. If the Grand Master, Deputy Grand Master, or Grand Wardens attend any funeral procession, they will take precedence, and preside over and conduct the ceremonies, unless they desire otherwise. Their place in the procession will be after the Master of the Lodge. Two Deacons, on the right and left, will attend a Grand Warden. When the Grand Master, or Deputy Grand Master, is present, the Book of Constitutions is borne before him, a Grand Sword Bearer follows him, and the Deacons, with black rods, are placed on his right and left, on a line, seven feet apart. If a Past Grand Officer appears in procession, he will be recognized with the customary respect.

ORDER OF PROCESSION.

The following Order of Procession will be proper to be observed, when a single Lodge conducts the ceremonies:

Tyler, with a drawn sword.

Stewards, with white rods.

Musicians, if they are Masons; otherwise in advance of the Tyler.

Marshal.

Master Masons.

Mark Masters.

Royal Arch Masons.

Select Masters.

Knights Templars.

Past Masters of the Lodge.

Senior and Junior Deacons.

Secretary and Treasurer.

Senior and Junior Wardens.

The Holy Writings on a Cushion, carried by the oldest or some suitable member of the Lodge.

The Master.

Clergy.

Pall Bearers.  Pall Bearers.

THE FUNERAL SERVICE.

The brethren being assembled at the Lodge-room, or some other convenient place, the presiding officer will open the Lodge on the third degree. After having stated the object of the meeting, the service will commence—all the brethren standing:

Master. Man that is born of a woman hath but a short time to live, and is full of misery. He cometh up, and is cut down like a flower; he fleeth as it were a shadow, and never continueth in one stay. In the midst of life we are in death. Of whom, then, may we seek for succor, but of THEE, O LORD, who for our sins art justly displeased?

My brethren, where is the man that liveth, that shall not see death?

Response by the brethren. Man walketh in a vain shadow: he heapeth up riches, and cannot tell who shall gather them.

Master. Where is now our departed brother?

Response. He dwelleth in night; he sojourneth in darkness.

Master. Can we offer any precious thing to redeem our brother?

Response. We have not the ransom. The place that once knew him shall know him no more for ever.

Master. Shall his name be lost upon earth?

Response. We wjll treasure it in our memories, we will record it in our hearts.

Master. How then will it be known?

Response. It shall live in the exercise of his virtues.

Master. When our brother died, did he carry nothing away with him?

Response. He fulfilled his destiny: Naked came he into this world, and naked he has departed out of it.

Master. Hear then the conclusion of the whole matter: *It is the* LORD *only that can give, and it is the* LORD *that hath taken away.*

Response. Blessed forever be the name of the LORD.

Master. Let us endeavor to live the life of the righteous, that our last end may be like his.

Response. God is our God for ever and ever. He will be our guide and our support, even through the dark valley of the shadow of death.

Master. I heard a voice from Heaven, saying unto me: "Write, from henceforth, blessed are the dead who die in the Lord; even so, saith the Spirit, for they rest from their labors."

The Master here takes the *roll,* on which is inscribed the name and age of the deceased, and says:

ALMIGHTY FATHER! in thy hands we leave, with humble submission, the soul of our departed brother,

The brethren will answer three times, giving the grand honors each time:

The will of GOD is accomplished. So be it.

The Master here deposits the *roll,* and repeats the following, or some other suitable prayer:

Most glorious and merciful Lord God, Author of all good, and Giver of every perfect gift; pour down, we implore Thee, thy blessing upon us: and under the deep solemnities of this occasion, bind us yet closer together in the ties of brotherly love and affection. May the present instance of mortality sensibly remind us of our approaching fate, and may it have an influence to wean our affections from the things of this transitory world, and to fix them more devotedly upon Thee, the only sure refuge in time of need. And at last, Great Parent of the Universe, when our journey shall be near its end; when the silver cord shall be loosed, and the golden bowl be broken; oh! in that moment of mortal extremity, may the "lamp of thy love" dispel the gloom of the dark valley; and may we be enabled to "work an entrance" into the Celestial Lodge above, and in thy glorious presence, amidst its ineffable mysteries, enjoy a union with the souls of our departed friends, perfect as is the happiness of Heaven, and durable as the eternity of God. Amen. So mote it be.

[The above ceremonies may be performed either at the Lodge, the house of the deceased, or in the church edifice, if the corpse be taken there, and religious services be performed. If at the house of the deceased, the Master will take his station at the head of the coffin, which will be uncovered, the Wardens at the foot, and the brethren around it, and commence as above prescribed. At the conclusion the coffin will be closed. If in the church, immediately after the benediction, the Master, Wardens, and brethren will place themselves as above directed, when the ceremonies will be commenced.]

A procession will then again be formed, and march to the place of interment in the order prescribed. The members of the Lodge will form a circle round the grave. The clergy and officers will take their station at the head, and the mourners at the foot, when the service will be resumed by the Master, as follows:

"The hand of the Lord was upon me, and carried me out in the Spirit of the Lord, and set me down in the midst of the valley which was full of bones.

"And caused me to pass by them round about: and behold, there were very many in the open valley; and lo, they were very dry.

"And he said unto me, Son of Man, can these bones live? And I answered, O Lord God, thou knowest.

"Again he said unto me, prophesy upon these bones, and say unto them, O ye dry bones, hear the word of the Lord,

"Thus saith the Lord God unto these bones: Behold, I will cause breath to enter into you, and ye shall live:

"And I will lay sinews upon you, and will bring up flesh upon you, and cover you with skin, and put breath in you, and *ye shall live;* and ye shall know that I am the Lord.

"So I prophesied as I was commanded; and as I prophesied there was a noise, and behold, a shaking, and the bones came together bone to his bone.

"And when I beheld, lo! the sinews and the flesh

came upon them, and the skin covered them above: but there was no breath in them.

"Then said He unto me, prophesy unto the wind; prophesy, Son of Man, and say to the wind, Thus saith the Lord God, Come from the four winds, O breath, and breathe upon these slain, that they may live.

"So I prophesied as he commanded me, and the breath came into them, and *they lived,* and stood upon their feet."

My Brethren: We are again called upon by a most solemn admonition to regard the uncertainty of human life, the immutable certainty of death, and the vanity of all earthly pursuits. Decripitude and decay are written in every living thing. The cradle and the coffin stand in juxtaposition to each other; and it is a melancholy truth, that so soon as we begin to live, that móment also we begin to die. Weakness and imperfection are the incidents of our fallen condition; the damp, dark grave is our destiny and our doom. What an eloquent commentary is here exhibited upon the instability of every human pursuit; and how touchingly does it echo the sad sentiment of the great preacher, who wrote for our perpetual warning, the immortal text, *Vanity of vanities, all is vanity.*

The last offices that we pay to the dead are useless things except as they constitute lessons to the living. The cold, marble form enclosed in the "narrow house" before you, is alike insensible to our sorrows and our ceremonies. It matters not now to him, whether two or three gather around the grave to perform his funeral ritual; or that hundreds have assembled, with the banners and insignia of our Order, to deposite him in his final resting place. It is of little moment how, or in what manner, his obsequies are performed; whether the wild winds chant his requiem, or it be accompanied with rare and costly music, and the minstrelsy of many voices. He has gone to accomplish the fearful destiny of all our race, and his body, in the profound slumber of the grave, to be desolved into its original elements.

What, then, are all the externals of human dignity, the power of wealth, the dreams of ambition, the pride of intellect, or the charms of beauty, when nature has paid her just debt? Fix your eyes on the last sad scene, and view humanity stript of its dazzling, meretricious ornaments; and you must needs be persuaded of the utter emptiness of these delusions. The monarch of an hundred provinces, at whose bidding nations pay obeisance, and the poor beggar that shivers at his gate, are *equals* in the house of death. The one is obliged to part with his sceptre and his crown—the other has no further use for his wallet and his rags—and both are indebted to their Mother Earth for a common sepulchre. In the grave all fallacies are detected, all ranks are leveled, and all distinctions are done away.

While we drop the sympathetic tear over the grave of our departed brother, let us cast around his foibles, whatever they may have been, the *broad mantle of a Mason's charity*, nor withhold from his memory the commendation that his virtues claim at our hands. It is of record, in the volume of Eternal Truth, that perfection on earth can never be attained. The best of created men did most grievously err, and the wisest of our race went sadly estray. Suffer, then, the apologies of human nature to plead in behalf of him who cannot any longer extenuate for himself.

The following invocations are then made:

Master. May we be true and faithful to each other, and may we live and die in love.

Response. So mote it be.

Master. May we profess what is good, and always act agreeably to our profession.

Response. So mote it be.

Master. May the Lord bless us and keep us; may the Lord be gracious unto us, and may all our good intentions be crowned with success.

Response. So mote it be.

Master. Glory be to God in the highest: on earth peace, and good will towards men.

Response. So mote it be; now, henceforth, and for ever. Amen.

The service is then resumed by the Master, as follows:

I am the ressurrection and the life, saith the Lord; he that believeth in me, though he were dead, yet shall he live; and whosoever liveth and believeth in me *shall never die.*

Here the apron is taken from the coffin and handed to the Master, and the corpse is made ready to be laid in the earth, when the service is resumed:

Forasmuch as it has pleased Almighty God, in his wise Providence, to take out of the world the soul of our deceased brother, we therefore commit his body to the ground. [*Here deposit the coffin.*] Earth to earth, ashes to ashes, dust to dust; looking for a general resurrection in the last day, when the earth and the sea shall give up their dead.

The Secretary will then advance and deposit the *roll* in the grave with the usual form.

Master. Friend and brother! we bid thee a *last,* a *long* FAREWELL! Thou art at rest from thy labors; may it be in peace!

Response. Amen. So mote it be.

If circumstances will permit, it will be proper at this stage of the proceedings, to sing the following, or some other appropriate Hymn; or it may be repeated by the Master, or omitted entirely, as shall be considered best:

FUNERAL HYMN.

compass the tomb, The Saviour has passed thro' its
world by thy side; But the wide arms of mer-cy are
doubt lingered long; But the sunshine of heaven beamed
guardian and guide; He gave thee, and took thee, and

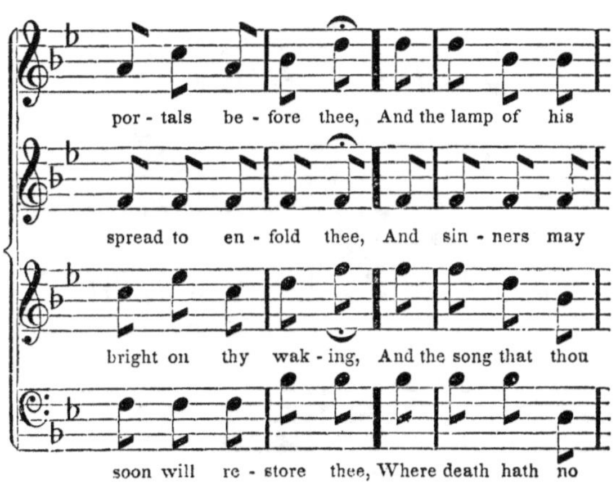
por - tals be - fore thee, And the lamp of his
spread to en - fold thee, And sin - ners may
bright on thy wak - ing, And the song that thou
soon will re - store thee, Where death hath no

love is thy guide through the gloom, And the
hope since the Sa - viour hath died, And the
heardst was the ser - a - phim's song, And
sting, since the Sa - viour hath died, Where

lamp of his love is thy guide thro' the gloom.
sin - ners may hope since the Sa - viour hath died.
song that thou heardst was the ser - a-phim's song.
death hath no sting, since the Sa - viour hath died.

The service is then resumed by the Master, who, presenting the *apron*, says,

This Lambskin, or white Apron, is an emblem of Innocence, and the badge of a Mason. It is more ancient than the Golden Fleece or the Roman Eagle; more honorable than the Star and Garter.

The Master then deposits it in the grave.

This emblem I now deposit in the grave of our deceased brother. By this we are reminded of the universal domination of Death. The arm of friendship cannot interpose to prevent his coming; the wealth of the world cannot purchase our release; nor will the innocence of youth, or the charms of beauty propitiate his purpose. The mattock, the coffin, and the melancholy grave, admonish us of our mortality, and that, sooner or later, these frail, weak bodies must moulder in their parent dust.

The Master, holding the *evergreen* in his hand, continues:

This Evergreen is an emblem of our faith in the immortality of the soul. By this we are reminded of our high and glorious destiny beyond the "world of shadows," and that there dwells within our tabernacle of clay, an imperishable, immortal spirit, over which the grave has no dominion, and death no power.

The brethren will now move in procession round

the place of interment, and severally drop the sprig of evergreen in the grave; after which the *public grand honors* are given. The Master then continues the ceremony in the following words:

From time immemorial, it has been the custom among the fraternity of Free and Accepted Masons, at the request of a brother, to accompany his corpse to the place of interment, there to deposit it with the usual formalities.

In conformity to this ancient usage, and at the request of our deceased brother, we have assembled at this time, in the character of Masons, to offer up, before the world, the last tribute of our affection; and thereby to demonstrate, in the strongest possible manner, the sincerity of our past esteem for him, and our steady attachment to the principles of the Order.

To those of his immediate relatives and friends, who are most heart-stricken at the loss we have all sustained, we have nothing of this world's consolation to offer. We can only sincerely, deeply, and most affectionately, sympathize with them in their afflictive bereavement. But, in the beautiful spirit of the Christian's theology, we dare to say, that He who "tempers the wind to the shorn lamb," looks down with infinite compassion upon the widow and fatherless in the hour of their desolation; and that the same benevolent Saviour, who wept while here on earth, will fold the arms of His love and protection around those who put their trust and confidence in HIM.

Then let us each, in our respective spheres, so improve this solemn warning of our God, that at last, when the "sheeted dead" are stirring, when the "great white throne" is set, and the volume of the record of our lives is opened, we may receive from the Omniscient Eternal Judge, the thrilling invitation, "Come, ye blessed of My Father, inherit the kingdom prepared for you from the foundation of the world."

The service is concluded with the following, or some other suitable Prayer:

Almighty and most merciful God, in whom we live, and move, and have our being, and before whom all men must appear to render an account for the deeds done in the body; we do most earnestly beseech Thee, as we now surround the grave of our fallen brother, to impress deeply upon our minds the solemnities of this day. May we ever remember that "in the midst of life we are in death," and so live and act our several parts as we will desire to have done, when the hour of our departure is at hand.

And oh! Gracious Father, vouchsafe us, we pray Thee, thy Divine assistance, to redeem our misspent time; and in the discharge of the duties thou hast assigned us, in the erection of our moral edifice, may we have *wisdom* from on high to direct us; *strength* commensurate with our task to support us; and the *beauty* of holiness to adorn and render all our performances acceptable in Thy sight. And at last, when our work on earth is done, when the *mallet* of death shall call us from *our labors*, may we obtain a blessed and everlasting rest in that Spiritual House, not made with hands, eternal in the Heavens.

Amen. So mote it be.

The procession will then return to the place whence it set out, where the necessary duties are complied with, and the Lodge is closed in the third degree.

CONSTITUTIONS.

The following "Ancient Constitutions are obligatory, as fundamental regulations, in all parts of the world," and it is therefore highly important that they should be accessible to every Mason. To accomplish this more fully, it has been thought advisable to include them in the present volume.

CHAPTER I.

OF THOSE WHO WOULD BE FREE AND ACCEPTED MASONS.

Before we enter upon the duties of the *operative Mason*, in the various offices to which he may be called in the Lodge, it is proper to give some account of what is absolutely requisite in all who aspire to partake of the sublime honors of those who are duly initiated into the mysteries and instructed in the art of ancient masonry.

Section First.

OF GOD AND RELIGION.

Whoever, from love of knowledge, interest, or curiosity, desires to be a Mason, is to know that, as his foundation and great corner stone, he is firmly to believe in the eternal God, and to pay that worship which is due to Him as the great Architect and Governor of the Universe.

A Mason must observe the moral law. And if he rightly understand the royal art, he will never be an atheist, or an irreligious *libertine;* and will never act against the great inward light of his own conscience.

He will likewise shun the errors of bigotry and superstition; making a due use of his own reason, according to that liberty wherewith a Mason is made free: for though in ancient times, Masons were charged to comply with the religious opinions and usages of the country or nation where they sojourned or worked, yet it is now thought most expedient that the brethren in general should only be charged to adhere to the essentials of religion, in which all men agree; leaving each brother to his own judgment as to particular forms. Whence being good men and true, of unsullied honor and unfailing honesty, the Order becomes the center of union, and the means of conciliating true friendship.

Section Second.

OF GOVERNMENT, AND THE CIVIL MAGISTRATE.

Whoever would be a true Mason is farther to know, that, by the privileges of his Order, his obligations as a subject and citizen will not be relaxed, but enforced. He is to be a lover of peace, and obedient to the civil powers which yield him protection, and are set over him, where he resides or works. Nor can a real Craftsman ever be concerned in conspiracies against the State, or be disrespectful to the magistrate; because the welfare of his country is his most happy object.

Now if any brother, forgetting for a time the rules of his craft, and listening to evil councils, should unhappily fall into a contrary conduct, he is not to be countenanced in his crimes or rebellion against the State; but he forfeits all the benefits of the Lodge, and his fellows will refuse to associate or converse with him in private, while he continues in his guilt; that no offence may be given to lawful government. Such a person, however, is still considered as a Mason, his title hitherto being indefeasible; and hopes are to be entertained, and endeavors used, that the rules of the craft may again recover him to his duty.

From the constant desire of true Masons, to adorn the countries where they reside with all useful arts, crafts, and improvements, they have been, from the earliest ages, encouraged and protected by the wisest rulers of States and Commonwealths; who have likewise thought it an honor to have their names enrolled among the fraternity, and have become the patrons of the Craft. And thus masonry, having alway flourished most in the peaceable times of every country, and having suffered in a particular manner through the calamitous effects of war, the craftsmen are the more strongly engaged and inclined to act agreeably to the prime principles of their art, in following *peace* and *love*, as far as possible, with all men.

And as political affairs have occasioned discord amongst the nearest relations and most intimate friends, Masons are enjoined never to speak of, or discuss them in the Lodge.

Section Third.

OF PRIVATE DUTIES.

Whoever would be a Mason should know how to practice all the private virtues. He should avoid all manner of *intemperance* or excess, which might prevent his performance of the laudable duties of his craft, or lead him into enormities, which would reflect dishonor upon the ancient fraternity. He is to be industrious in his profession, and true to the Lord and Master he serves. He is to labor *justly*, and not to eat any man's bread for nought; but to pay truly for his meat and drink. What leisure his labor allows, he is to employ in studying the arts and sciences with a diligent mind, that he may the better perform all his duties to his Creator, his country, his neighbor, and himself.

He is to seek and acquire, as far as possible, the virtues of *patience, meekness, self-denial, forbearance*, and the like; which give him the command over himself, and enable him to govern his own family with affection, dignity, and prudence; at the same time checking every disposition injurious to the world, and promoting that love and service which brethren of the same household owe to each other.

Therefore, to afford succor to the distressed, to divide

our bread with the industrious poor, and to put the misguided traveller into the way, are duties of the craft, suitable to the dignity, and expressive of its usefulness. But though a Mason is never to shut his ear unkindly against the complaints of any of the human race, yet, when a brother is oppressed or suffers, he is in a more peculiar manner called to open his whole soul in love and compassion to him, and to relieve him without prejudice, according to his capacity.

It is also necessary, that all who would be true Masons should learn to abstain from all malice, slander, and evil speaking; from all provoking, reproachful and ungodly language; keeping always a tongue of good report.

A Mason should know how to obey those who are set over him, however inferior they may be in worldly rank or condition. For although masonry divests no man of his honors and titles, yet in the Lodge, pre-eminence of virtue, and knowledge in the royal art, are considered as the true source of all nobility, rule and government.

The virtue indispensably requisite in Masons, is secrecy. This is the guard of their confidence, and the security of their trust. So great stress is to be laid upon it, that it is enforced under the strongest penalties and obligations; nor is their esteem in any man to be accounted *wise*, who has not intellectual strength and ability sufficient to cover and conceal such honest secrets as are committed to him, as well as his own more serious and private affairs.

Section Fourth.

OF PREREQUISITES.

No person is capable of becoming a member, unless, together with the virtues aforementioned, or at least a disposition to seek and acquire them, he is also free born; of mature and discreet age; of good report; of sufficient natural endowments, and the senses of a *man;* with an estate, office, trade, occupation, or some visible way of acquiring an honest livelihood, and of working in his craft, as becomes the members of this most ancient and honorable fraternity, who ought not only to earn what is sufficient for themselves and families, but likewise something to spare for works of charity, and supporting the true dignity of the Royal Craft. Every person desiring admission must also be upright in body, not deformed or dismembered, at the time of making; but of hale and entire limbs, as a *man* ought to be.

No brother shall propose for admission into this ancient and honorable society, any person through friendship or partiality, who does not possess the moral and social virtues, a sound head and a good heart; and who has not an entire exemption from all those ill qualities and vices, which would bring dishonor on the Craft.

Section Fifth.

INSTRUCTIONS FOR THE CANDIDATE.

A strict though private and impartial inquiry will be made into the character and ability of the candidate, before he can be admitted into any Lodge: and by the rules of masonry, no friend, who can wish to propose him, may show him any favor. But if he have a friend who is a Mason, and is every way satisfied, his duty is described as follows:

Section Sixth.

OF PROPOSING CANDIDATES.

Every person desirous of being made a Freeemason in any Lodge shall be proposed by a member, who shall give an account of the candidate's name, age, quality, title, trade, place of residence, description of his person, and other necessary requisites, as mentioned in the foregoing sections. And it is generally required, that such proposal be also seconded by some one or more members who are acquainted with the candidate. Such proposals shall also be made in Lodge hours, at least one Lodge night before initiation, in order that the brethren may have sufficient time and opportunity to make a strict inquiry into the morals, character, and circumstances of the candidate, for which purpose a special committee is sometimes appointed.

The brother who proposes a candidate shall, at the same time deposit such a sum of money for him as the rules or by-laws of the Lodge may require, which is forfeited to the Lodge if the candidate should not attend according to his proposal, but is to be returned to him if he should not be approved or elected. In case he be elected, he is to pay, in addition to his deposit, such further sum as the laws of the Lodge may require, and clothe the Lodge, or make some other present, as his circumstances will admit and the brethren agree to accept, for the benefit of the craft and distressed members.

Section Seventh.

THE CANDIDATE.

He has a right, before his admission, to desire his friend to show him the Warrant, or Dispensation, by which the Lodge is held; which, if genuine, he will find to be an instrument written or printed upon parchment, and signed by some Grand Master, his Deputy, the Grand Wardens and Grand Secretary, sealed with the Grand Lodge seal, constituting particular persons therein named, as Master and Wardens, with full power to congregate and hold a Lodge at such a place, and therein "make and admit Freemasons, according to the most ancient and honorable customs of the Royal Craft, in all ages and nations throughout the known world, with full power and authority to nominate and choose their successors," &c.

He may also request the perusal of the by-laws, which being short, he may read in the presence of his friend, and be shown a list of the members of the Lodge; by all which he will be better able to judge whether he could associate with them, and render a ready conformity to their rules. Being thus FREE to judge for himself, he will not be liable to the dangers of deception. But, on the contrary, will be admitted into a society where he may converse with men of honor and honesty —be exercised in all the offices of brotherly love, and be made acquainted with some things of which it is not lawful to speak or make known OUT OF THE LODGE.

Previously to his introduction, every candidate ought to subscribe the following declaration:

I, A. B., do seriously declare, upon my honor, that unbiassed by friends, and uninfluenced by unworthy motives, I freely and voluntarily offer myself a candidate for the mysteries of Freemasonry; that I am solely prompted by a favorable opinion conceived of the institution, a desire of knowledge, and a sincere wish to be serviceable to my fellow creatures; and that I will cheerfully conform to the ancient established usages and customs of the society.

"As witness my hand, this day of in the year A. D.

F. D. }
D. F. } Witnesses A. B."

CHAPTER II.

OF A LODGE AND ITS GOVERNMENT.

Section First.

OF A LODGE.

A *Lodge* is a place where Masons assemble and work: hence that assembly, or duly organized society of Masons, is called a *Lodge*, and every brother ought to belong to one, and to be subject to its by-laws and the general regulations. It is either particular or general, and will be best understood by attending it, and by the regulations of the General or Grand Lodge hereunto annexed. In ancient times, no Master or Fellow could be absent from it, especially when warned to appear at it, without incurring a severe censure, until it appeared to the Master and Wardens that pure necessity hindered him.

Section Second.

OF OFFICERS AND MEMBERS IN GENERAL.

A Lodge ought to assemble for work at least once in every calendar month; and must consist of one Master; two Wardens, senior and junior; one Secretary, one Treasurer, two Deacons, one or more Stewards, a Tyler, and as many members as the Master and the majority of the Lodge shall think proper; although more than forty or fifty, when they can attend regularly, as the wholesome rules of the craft require, are generally found inconvenient for working to advantage; and, therefore, when a Lodge comes to be thus numerous, some of the ablest Master workmen, and others under their direction, will obtain leave to separate and apply to the Grand Lodge for a Warrant to work by themselves, in order to the advancement of the craft, as the laws hereafter to be delivered will more particularly show.

Every member of a working Lodge should be a Master Mason.

Section Third.

OF THE MASTER—HIS ELECTION, OFFICE AND DUTY.

All preferment among Masons depends on real worth and personal merit only, that the society may be well served, and the Royal Craft maintained.

No brother should be a Master till he has first served a Lodge acceptably in the office of Warden, unless in extraordinary cases, or when a new Lodge is to be formed, and no Past or former Warden is to be found among the members. But, three Master Masons, although they have served in no such offices, if they be well learned, may be constituted Master and Wardens of such new Lodge, or of any old Lodge in the like emergency; and it shall be their duty first to qualify themselves thoroughly for their work.

The Master of every Lodge shall be annually chosen by ballot, on some stated Lodge night. Each member hath one vote. And when the ballot is closed, the former Master shall carefully examine the votes, and audibly declare him who hath the majority to be duly elected. In like manner shall the Lodge proceed in the choice of all other officers; great care being taken that none be put in nomination for favor or affection, birth, or fortune, exclusively of the consideration of real merit and ability to fill the office for the honor and advancement of masonry. No Mason chosen into any office can refuse to serve, unless he has served in the same office before. The Master of every regular Lodge, thus duly elected and installed, has it in special charge, as appurtenant to his office, duty and dignity, to see that all the by-laws of his Lodge, as well as the General Regulations from the Grand Lodge, be duly observed; that his Wardens discharge their office faithfully, and be examples of diligence and sobriety to the craft; that true and exact minutes and entries of all proceedings be made and kept by the Secretary; that the Treasurer keep and render exact and just accounts at the stated times, according to the by-laws and orders of the Lodge; and, in general, that all the goods and moneys belonging to the body be truly managed and dispensed, according to the vote and directions of the majority.

The Master shall also take care that no Apprentice or Fellow Craft be taken into his house or Lodge, unless he has sufficient employment for him, and finds him to be duly qualified, according to the rules before laid down, for learning and understanding the sublime mysteries of the Art. Thus shall apprentices be admitted, upon farther improvement, as Fellow Crafts; and, in due time, be raised to the sublime degree of Master Masons, animated with the prospect of passing in future through all the higher honors of masonry, viz: those of Wardens and Masters of their Lodges, and perhaps at length of Grand Wardens and Grand Masters of all the Lodges, according to their merit.

The Master of a particular Lodge has the right and authority of *calling* his Lodge, or congregating the members into a Chapter, at pleasure, upon the application of any of the brethren, and upon any emergency and occurrence which, in his judgment, may require their meeting; and he is to fill the chair when present. It is likewise his duty, together with his Wardens, to attend the Grand Lodge at the quarterly Communications; and such occasional or special Grand Communications as the good of the craft may require, when duly summoned by the Grand Secretary, and within such reasonable distance of the place of holding the Grand Lodge as the laws of the same may have ascertained. When in the Grand Lodge, and at general as well as special Communications, the Master and Wardens, or either of them, have full power and authority to represent their Lodge, and to transact all matters as well and truly as if the whole were there present.

The Master has the right of appointing some brother, who is most commonly the Secretary of the Lodge, to keep the book of by-laws, and other laws given to the Lodge by proper authority; and in this book shall also be kept the names of all the members of the Lodge, and a list of all the Lodges within the same Grand Communication, with the usual times and places of their meeting.

Section Fourth.

THE WARDENS OF A LODGE.

1. None but Master Masons can be Wardens of a Lodge.

2. The Senior Warden succeeds to all the duties of

the Master, and fills the chair when he is absent. If the Master goes abroad on business, resigns, or is deposed, the Senior Warden shall fill his place until the next stated time of election. And although it was formerly held, that in such cases the Master's authority ought to revert to the last Past Master who is present, yet it is now the settled rule, that the authority devolves upon the Senior Warden, and in his absence upon the Junior Warden, even although a former Master be present. But the Wardens will generally honor a Past Master that may be present, and will call on him to take the chair, upon the presumption of his experience and skill in conducting the business of the Lodge.

Nevertheless, such Past Master still holds his authority under the Senior Warden, and cannot act until he congregates the Lodge. If none of the officers be present, nor any former Master to take the chair, the members according to seniority and merit, shall fill the places of the absent officers.

The business of the Wardens in the Lodge is generally to assist the Master in conducting the business and managing the craft, in due order and form, when the Master is present. Particular Lodges do likewise, by their by-laws, assign particular duties to their Wardens for their own better government; which such Lodges have a right to do, provided they transgress not the old landmarks, nor in any degree violate the true genius and spirit of masonry.

Section Fifth.

OF THE SECRETARY OF A LODGE.

The Secretary shall keep a proper register or record of all transactions and proceedings of the Lodge, that are to be committed to writing; which shall be faithfully entered in the Lodge books, from the minutas taken in open Lodge, after being duly read, amended if necessary, and approved of before the close of every meeting; in order that the said transactions or authentic copies may be laid before the Grand Lodge once in every quarter if required.

In particular, the Secretary shall keep exact lists of all the members of the Lodge, with the admission of new members; and shall prepare and send to the Secretary of the Grand Lodge, the list of members, together with all expulsions and rejections for the time being, to the intent that the Grand Secretary, and consequently the members of the Grand Lodge, may be at all times enabled to know the names and number of members in each Lodge under their jurisdiction, with the hand writing of the different officers; and pay all due respect to the brethren recommended by them.

Section Sixth.

OF THE TREASURER OF A LODGE.

The Treasurer is to receive and keep exact accounts of all moneys raised, or paid according to rule, for the advancement of the Lodge and benefit of the brethren, and to pay all orders duly drawn upon him by the authority of the Lodge. He is to keep regular entries both of his receipts and expenses; and to have his books and vouchers always ready for examination at such stated times as the by-laws require, or when specially called upon by order of the Master and brethren.

The Treasurer is likewise to have the charge and custody of the chest, jewels, and furniture of the Lodge; unless when the Master and majority may judge it more convenient to appoint some other responsible brother for that particular duty; or when the officers of the Lodge may take the charge immediately upon themselves. But the Warrant or Charter is in the custody of the Master.

Section Seventh.

OF THE DEACONS OF A LODGE.

The Deacons are to assist the Master and Wardens in the execution of their duty, to examine and welcome visiting brethren, to prepare candidates, and to perform such other services as are assigned to them.

Section Eighth.

STEWARDS.

The Stewards are to provide refreshments, and make a regular report of the expense to the Treasurer; and to see that the regalia of the Lodge are in good order and always ready for use.

Section Ninth.

OF THE TYLER OF A LODGE.

In order that due decorum be observed, while the Lodge is engaged in what is serious and solemn, and for the preservation of secrecy and good harmony, a brother well skilled in the Master's part, shall be appointed and paid for tyling the Lodge door, during the time of communication. Generally a brother is to be preferred, to whom the fees of the office may be necessary and serviceable, on account of his particular circumstances.

His duty is fixed by custom, and known to every brother. He is to be true and trusty, and to obey the special directions of the Lodge.

Section Tenth.

OF THE NUMBER TO BE INITIATED.

No Lodge shall make more than *five* new brethren at one time, nor shall any person be made, or admitted a member of a Lodge, without being proposed at least *one Lodge night* before, unless in cases of emergency, or by dispensation from the Grand Master or his Deputy, in his absence, that due notice may be given to all the members for the necessary inquiries into the candidate's character; and that there may be *unanimity* in the election and admission of members.

Section Eleventh.

OF PRIVILEGES IN LODGES.

The majority of every particular Lodge, when duly congregated, have the privilege of instructing their Master and Wardens for their conduct in the Grand Lodge and Quarterly Communications; and all particular Lodges in the same Communication, shall, as much as possible, observe the same rules and usages; and appoint some of their members to visit each other in the different Lodges, as often as it may be convenient.

When it so happens that a Lodge cannot attend the Communications of the Grand Lodge, they may appoint a brother, who is a Master Mason, and of real merit, and give him instructions to represent them, and vote in their behalf. He bearing their certificate under the seal of the Lodge, and signed by the Master and Wardens, may, if approved by the officers of the Grand Lodge, take his seat among them, and vote and act in the name of the Lodge he represents. But no individual can appear for more than one Lodge at the same time.

Lodges shall have place according to the date of their constitution.

If any Lodge shall cease to meet regularly for twelve months successively, its charter shall be void.

CHAPTER III.

OF THE BEHAVIOUR OF MASONS, AS MEMBERS OF A LODGE.

1. OF ATTENDANCE.

Every brother ought to belong to some regular Lodge, and should always appear therein properly clothed, truly subjecting himself to all its by-laws and the general regulations. He must attend all meetings, when duly summoned, unless he can offer to the Master and Wardens such plea of necessity for his absence as the said laws and regulations may admit.

By the ancient rules and usages of masonry, which are generally adopted among the by-laws of every Lodge, no plea was judged sufficient to excuse any absentee, unless he could satisfy the Lodge that he was detained by some extraordinary and unforeseen necessity.

None have a right to vote in the Lodge but such as are members.

No brother shall be a member of more than one Lodge at the same time.

2. OF WORKING.

All Masons should work faithfully and honestly. All the working hours appointed by law, or confirmed by custom, are to be strictly observed. The usual hours of working are—"from seven o'clock in the evening until ten, between the 25th of March and the 25th of

September; and from six until nine, between the 25th of September and the 25th of March."

The Master and Masons shall faithfully finish their work.

None shall envy a brother's prosperity, or put him out of his work, if capable of finishing it.

All Masons shall receive their wages without murmuring. They must avoid all unbecoming modes of expression; and shall call each other brother in the Lodge.

3. OF BEHAVIOUR IN THE LODGE.

While the Lodge is open for work, Masons must hold no private conversation or committees, without leave from the Master; nor talk of any thing foreign or impertinent, nor interrupt the Master or Wardens, or any brother addressing himself to the chair; nor behave inattentively while the Lodge is engaged in what is serious and solemn; but every brother shall pay due reverence to the Master and Wardens, and all his fellows.

Every brother guilty of a fault, shall submit to the Lodge, unless he appeal to the Grand Lodge.

No private offences, or disputes about nations, families, religion, or politics, must be brought within the doors of the Lodge.

4. OF BEHAVIOUR AFTER THE LODGE IS CLOSED.

When the Lodge is closed, and the labor finished, the brethren, before they depart home to their rest, may enjoy themselves with innocent mirth, enlivened and exalted with their own peculiar songs and sublime pieces of music; but avoiding all *excess*, considering each other, in the hours both of labor and festivity, as always free. And therefore no brother is to be hindered from going home when he pleases; for although, after Lodge hours, Masons are as other men, yet if they should fall into excess, the blame, though unjustly, may be cast upon the fraternity, by the ignorant or the envious.

CHAPTER IV.

OF THE BEHAVIOUR OF MASONS, IN THEIR PRIVATE CHARACTER.

1. WHEN A NUMBER OF BRETHREN HAPPEN TO MEET, WITHOUT ANY STRANGER AMONG THEM, AND NOT IN A LODGE.

In such case, you are to salute each other in a courteous manner, as you are or may be instructed in the Lodge, and freely communicate hints of knowledge, but without disclosing secrets, unless to those who have given proof of their taciturnity and honor. Masonry divests no man of the honors due to him before, or that may become due after he was made a Mason. On the contrary, it increases respect, teaching us to add to all his other honors, those which as Masons we cheerfully pay to an eminent brother, distinguishing him above all of his rank and station, and serving him readily according to our ability.

2. WHEN IN THE PRESENCE OF STRANGERS, WHO ARE NOT MASONS.

Before those who are not Masons, you must be cautious in your words and carriage; so that the most penetrating stranger shall not be able to discover what is not proper to be intimated. The impertinent and ensnaring questions, or ignorant and idle discourse of those who seek to pry into the secrets and mysteries of the craft, must be prudently answered and managed, or the discourse wisely diverted to another subject, as your discretion and duty shall direct.

3. WHEN AT HOME, AND IN YOUR NEIGHBORHOOD.

Masons ought to be moral men. Consequently they should be good husbands, good parents, good sons, and good neighbors; avoiding all excess injurious to themselves or families, and wise as to all affairs, both of their own household and of the Lodge, for certain reasons known to themselves.

4. OF BEHAVIOUR TOWARDS A FOREIGN BROTHER, OR STRANGER.

You are cautiously to examine a stranger or foreign brother, as prudence and the rules of the craft direct, that you may not be imposed upon by a pretender; and if you discover any one to be such, you are to reject him, but with proper caution. But such as are found to be true and faithful, you are to respect as brothers, relieving them, if in want, to your utmost power, or directing them how to find relief; and employing them, if you can, or else recommending them to employment.

5. OF BEHAVIOUR TOWARDS A BROTHER, WHETHER PRESENT OR ABSENT.

Free and Accepted Masons have ever been charged to avoid all slander of true and faithful brethren, with all malice and unjust resentment, or talking disrespectfully of a brother's person or performance. Nor must they suffer any to spread unjust reproaches or calumnies against a brother behind his back, nor to injure him in his fortune, occupation or character; but they shall defend such a brother, and give him notice of any danger or injury wherewith he may be threatened, to enable him to escape the same, as far as is consistent with honor, prudence, and the safety of religion, morality, and the State, but no farther.

6. CONCERNING DIFFERENCES AND LAWSUITS, IF ANY SUCH SHOULD UNHAPPILY ARISE AMONG BRETHREN.

If a brother do you an injury, or if you have any difference with him about any worldly or temporal business, or interest, apply first to your own or his Lodge, to have the matter in dispute adjusted by the brethren. And if either brother be not satisfied with the determination of the Lodge, an appeal may be made to the Grand Lodge; and you are never to enter into a lawsuit until the matter cannot be decided as above. And if it be a matter that wholly concerns masonry, lawsuits are to be entirely avoided, and the good advice of prudent brethren is to be followed, as they are the best referees of such differences.

But where references are either impracticable or unsuccessful, and courts of law or equity must at last decide, you must still follow the general rules of masonry, avoiding all wrath, malice, rancor, and personal ill will, in carrying on the suit with a brother; neither saying or doing any thing to prevent the continuance or renewal of that brotherly love and friendship, which are the glory and cement of this ancient fraternity. Thus shall we show to all the world the benign influence of masonry, as wise, true and faithful brethren have done from the beginning of time; and as all who shall follow us, and would be thought worthy of that name, will continue to do.

☞These charges, and such others as shall be given to you, *in a way that cannot be written,* you are strictly and conscientiously to observe; and, that they may be the better observed, they should be read or made known to new brethren at their *making;* and at other times, as the Master shall direct. *Amen.*

CHAPTER V.

Section First.

OF GRAND LODGES IN GENERAL.

A Grand Lodge consists of the Masters and Wardens of all the regular Lodges within its jurisdiction, with the Grand Master at their head, the Deputy Grand Master on his left, and the Grand Wardens in their proper places; attended also by the Grand Secretary, Grand Treasurer, Grand Marshal, Grand Sword Bearer, Grand Tyler, Grand Pursuivant, and other necessary officers, as will be explained in the proper place; all of whom must be Master Masons.

No new Lodge is acknowledged, nor can their officers be admitted into the Grand Lodge, until such new Lodge is first regularly *constituted*, and registered by the authority of the Grand Lodge.

All Past Grand Masters, Past Deputy Grand Masters, and Past Grand Wardens, are considered as members of, and admitted to vote in all Grand Lodges. By courtesy, as well as custom, Past Masters, Past Grand Secretaries, and Past Grand Treasurers, have the privilege of sitting in all the Grand Lodges, and voting in such matters, as by the rules of the Grand Lodge, they might or could have voted in, while in office.

No Master, Warden, or other member of the Grand Lodge, should ever attend the same, without the jewels which he ought to wear in his own particular Lodge, except for some good and sufficient reason to be allowed of by the Grand Lodge. And when the officer of any particular Lodge, from such urgent business, or necessity, as may regularly plead his excuse, cannot personally attend the Grand Lodge, he may nominate and send a brother of his Lodge, with his jewel and clothing, to supply his room, and to support the honor of his Lodge in the Grand Lodge.

A brother of eminence, and of the rank of Master, having business, or whose attendance is necessary in any point of evidence or intelligence, may be admitted into the Grand Lodge upon motion, or leave asked and given; but such brother, thus admitted, shall have no vote, nor be allowed to speak to any question without leave, or unless desired to give his opinion.

The Grand Lodge shall meet four times a year statedly, for Quarterly Communications, and should also have occasional meetings and adjournments, monthly or otherwise, as business may require; and such meeting shall be held in the hall of the Grand Lodge, unless for some particular reason the Grand Master should think fit to appoint some other place of special meeting.

All matters in the Grand Lodge shall be determined by a majority of votes, each member having one vote, unless the Grand Lodge leave any particular thing to the determination of the Grand Master.

The business of the Grand Lodge, whether at Quarterly Communications or other meetings, is seriously to communicate and consider, transact and settle, all matters that concern the prosperity of the craft and the fraternity in general, or private Lodges and brethren in particular. Thus all differences that cannot be accommodated privately, nor by a particular Lodge, are to be seriously eonsidered and decided. And if any brother thinks himself aggrieved by such decision, he may, by lodging an appeal in writing with the Grand Secretary, have the matter reheard and finally determined upon at the next ensuing Quarterly Communication, provided it be not the annual Grand Lodge, or the feast days of St. John; on which, by the new and wise regulations, it is agreed and ordered that no petitions or appeals should be heard, or any business transacted, that tends to interrupt the harmony of the assembly; but all shall be referred to the next meeting of the Grand Lodge. And, in general, whatever business cannot be transacted or finished at any one meeting of the Grand Lodge, may either be adjourned to the next, or referred to a proper committee, to be by them heard, considered and reported upon to the said next meeting.

The officers of all private Lodges, under the jurisdiction of the Grand Lodge, shall, at every Quarterly Communication, (except the distant Lodges, which shall annually on or before the festival of Saint John the Evangelist,) deliver an exact list of such members as have been made, or even admitted by them, since the last preceding Communication; and books shall be kept in the Grand Lodge, by some able brother to be appointed Grand Secretary, in which the said lists and returns shall be duly recorded; together with all the Lodges in Communication, the usual times and places of their assembly, and the names of all their members. In the said books are also to be registered all the proceedings, and other affairs of the Grand Lodge, *which are proper to be written.*

The Grand Lodge shall likewise consider of the most prudent and effectual means of collecting and managing what money may accrue to the general charity fund.

Section Second.

OF THE ELECTION OF THE GRAND MASTER.

The Grand Lodge must meet in some convenient place in order to elect new or re-appoint the old officers; and such election or re-appointment shall be made in such season that the Grand Lodge may be completely organized, and duly prepared for the celebration of the annual feast in June, and other important business of the season.

The election shall be made either by holding up of hands, or by ballot, as may be agreed by the majority, on motion made and seconded for that purpose; provided always that the brother recommended by the Grand Master in office, as his successor, be the first voted for, either by holding up of hands, or by ballot, and if he is not chosen, the other candidates in the order they were proposed, until one has the majority of voices or ballots. When the election is thus made, he is to be proclaimed, installed and saluted, if present; but if not present, a day is to be appointed for this ceremony. The ceremony of installing the new Grand Master is to be conducted by the last Grand Master; but he may, nevertheless, order any brother well skilled in the ceremony to assist him, or act as his deputy on the occasion.

In case the new Grand Master, when nominated or chosen, cannot attend at the time appointed for his instalment, he may be installed by proxy, on signifying his acceptance of the office; but such proxy must be either the last or a former Grand Master, or else a very reputable Past Master.

Section Third.

OF THE ELECTION OR APPOINTMENT OF THE DEPUTY GRAND MASTER.

The last Grand Master thus continued, or a new Grand Master thus appointed and installed, hath an inherent right to nominate and appoint the Deputy Grand Master; because, as the Grand Master cannot be supposed to be able to give his attendance on every emergency, it hath been always judged necessary, not only to allow him a Deputy, but that such Deputy should be a person in whom he can perfectly confide, and with whom he can have full harmony.

Section Fourth.

OF THE GRAND WARDENS.

The Grand Lodge has the right of electing the Grand

Wardens; and any member has a right to propose one or both the candidates, either the old Wardens or new ones; and the two persons who have the majority of votes or ballots, are declared duly elected.

Section Fifth.

OF THE GRAND SECRETARY.

The office of Grand Secretary hath become one of great importance to the Grand Lodge. All the transactions of the Lodge are to be drawn into form, and duly recorded by him. All petitions, applications and appeals are to pass through his hands. No warrant, certificate, or instrument of writing from the Grand Lodge, is authentic without his attestation and signature, and his affixing the grand seal as the laws require. The general correspondence with Lodges and brethren over the whole world is to be managed by him, agreeably to the voice of the Grand Lodge, and directions of the Grand Master or his Deputy, whom he must, therefore, be always ready to attend, with the books of the Lodge, in order to give all necessary information concerning the general state of matters, and what is proper to be done upon any emergency.

For these reasons, at every annual election or appointment of Grand Officers, the nomination or appointment of the Grand Secretary has been considered as the right of the Grand Master, being properly his amanuensis, and an officer as necessary to him as his Deputy. But in America, Grand Masters, not being tenacious of prerogative, have relinquished this privilege, and the Grand Secretary is chosen by nomination and vote of the Grand Lodge.

The Grand Secretary, by virtue of his office, is a member of the Grand Lodge, and may sit down and vote accordingly.

The Grand Secretary may have an assistant, with the consent of the Grand Lodge; but he will not be considered as a member, nor admitted to vote.

Section Sixth.

OF THE ELECTION AND OFFICE OF GRAND TREASURER.

The Grand Treasurer is elected by the body of the Grand Lodge, in the same manner as the Grand Wardens; he being considered as an officer peculiarly responsible to all the members in due form assembled, as having the charge of their common stock and property. To him is committed the care of all money raised for the general charity, and other uses of the Grand Lodge, an account of which he is regularly to enter in a book, with the respective uses for which the several sums are intended. He is likewise to pay out, or expend the same on such orders, signed as the rules of the Grand Lodge in this respect shall allow to be valid.

The Grand Treasurer, by virtue of his office, is a member of the Grand Lodge. He shall always be present in the Lodge, and ready to attend the Grand Master, and other Grand Officers, with his books for inspection when required; and likewise any committee that may be appointed for adjusting and examining his accounts.

Section Seventh.

OF THE GRAND TYLER AND GRAND PURSUIVANT.

These officers of the Grand Lodge must be Master Masons, but none of them are members of the Grand Lodge. The Tyler's duty is to attend at the door, to see that none but members enter into the Lodge.

The business of the Pursuivant is to stand at the inward door of the Grand Lodge, and to report the names and titles of all that want admittance, as given to him by the Tyler. He is also to go upon messages and perform other services known in the Lodge.

☞The Grand Deacons, whose duty is well known in the Grand Lodge, as particular assistants to the Grand Master and Senior Warden, in conducting the business of the Lodge, are always members of the same; and may be either nominated occasionally on every Lodge night, or appointed annually.

Section Eighth.

GENERAL RULES FOR CONDUCTING THE BUSINESS OF THE GRAND LODGE, IN CASES OF THE ABSENCE OF ANY OF THE GRAND OFFICERS.

If the Grand Master is absent at any meeting of the Grand Lodge, stated or occasional, the Deputy is to supply his place.

If the Deputy is likewise absent, the Senior Grand Warden takes the Chair, and in his absence the Junior Grand Warden. All Grand Officers, Present and Past, take place of every Master of a Lodge, and the present Grand Officers take place of all Past Grand Officers. Nevertheless, any of them may resign their privilege, to do honor to any eminent brother or Past Master, whom the Lodge may be willing to place in the chair on any particular occasion.

If the Grand Officers are not present at any Grand Lodge duly summoned, the Master of the Senior Private Lodge who may be present, is to take the chair, although there may be Masters of Lodges present who are older Masons.

But to prevent disputes, the Grand Master, when he finds he must be necessarily absent from any Grand Lodge, usually gives a special commission, under his hand and seal of office, countersigned by the Grand Secretary, to the Senior Grand Warden, or in his absence to the Junior, or in case of the absence of both, to any other Grand Officer, or particular Master of a Lodge, Past or Present, to supply his place, if the Deputy Grand Master be necessarily absent.

But if there be no special commission, the general rule of precedence is that the Junior Grand Warden supplies the place of the Senior in his absence; and if both are absent, the oldest former Grand Wardens take place immediately, and act as Grand Wardens *pro tempore,* unless they resign their privilege.

When neither the Grand Wardens of the present, nor of any former year, are in company, the Grand Master, or he that legally presides in his stead, calls forth whom he pleases, to act as Deputy Grand Master and Grand Wardens, although the preference is generally given to the Master or Past Master of the oldest Lodge present. The presiding grand officer has the further privilege of appointing a Secretary or any other grand officer, if neither the stated officers, nor the deputies of such of them as have a right to nominate a deputy, be present.

In case of the death of a Grand Master, the same order of succession and precedency takes place, as above set forth, until a new Grand Master is duly chosen, and installed.

Old Grand Officers may be again chosen officers of private Lodges, and this does not deprive them of any of the privileges to which, as old Grand Officers, they are entitled in the Grand Lodge; only, an old Grand Officer, being the officer of a private Lodge, must depute a past officer of his particular Lodge to act for him in the Grand Lodge, when he ascends to his former rank in the same.

Section Ninth.

OF GRAND VISITATIONS, COMMUNICATIONS, ANNUAL FEASTS, &C.

The Grand Master, with his Deputy, the Grand Wardens, and Grand Secretary, shall, if possible, annually go at least once round, and visit all the Lodges under his jurisdiction; or, when this laudable duty becomes impracticable, from the extent of his jurisdiction and large number of Lodges, he shall, as often as necessary, and if possible, annually, appoint visiters of different districts, composed of his Grand Officers, and such other assistants as he may think proper, who shall make faithful report of their proceedings to the Grand Lodge, according to the instructions given them.

When both the Grand Master and Deputy Grand Master are absent, the Senior or Junior Grand Warden may preside as Deputy in visiting Lodges, or in constituting any new Lodge.

The brethren of all the regular Lodges, in the same general jurisdiction and Grand Communication, shall meet in some convenient place on St. John's day, to celebrate their festival; either in their own or any other regular Lodge, as they shall judge most convenient. And any brethren who are found true and faithful members of the Ancient Craft, may be admitted. But only those who are members of the Grand Lodge must be present during the installation of Grand Officers.

CHAPTER VI.

Section First.

GENERAL REGULATIONS OF ANCIENT YORK MASONS.

I. The Grand Master, or Deputy, has full authority and right, not only to be present, but also to preside in every Lodge, with the Master of the Lodge on his left hand: and to order his Grand Wardens to attend him, who are not to act as Wardens of particular Lodges, but in his presence and at his command; for the Grand Master while in a particular Lodge, may command the Wardens of that Lodge, or any other Master Masons, to act as his Wardens, *pro tempore.*

II. The Master of a particular Lodge has the right and authority of congregating the members of his Lodge into a Chapter, upon any emergency or occurrence, as well as to appoint the time and place of their usual forming; and in case of death or sickness, or necessary absence of the Master, the Senior Warden shall act as Master *pro tempore*, if no brother is present who has been Master of that Lodge before; for the absent Master's authority reverts to the last Master present; though he connot act till the Senior Warden congregates the Lodge.

III. The Master of each particular Lodge, or one of the Wardens, or some other brother, by appointment of the Master, shall keep a book, containing their by-laws, the names of their members, and a list of all the Lodges in town, with the usual times and places of their forming, and also the transactions of their own Lodge, that are proper to be written.

IV. No Lodge shall make more than five new brothers at one and the same time, without an urgent necessity; nor any man under the age of twenty-five years, who must be also his own master, unless by a dispensation from the Grand Master.

V. No man can be accepted a member of a particular Lodge without previous notice one month before given to the Lodge, in order to make due enquiry into the reputation and capacity of the candidate, unless by a dispensation.

VI. But no man can be entered a brother in any particular Lodge, or admitted a member thereof, without the unanimous consent of all the members of that Lodge then present, when the candidate is proposed; and when their consent is formally asked by the Master, they are to give their consent in their own prudent way, either virtually or in form, but with unanimity; nor is this inherent privilege subject to a dispensation, because the members of a particular Lodge are the best judges of it; and because, if a turbulent member should be imposed on them, it might spoil their harmony, or hinder the freedom of their communication, or even break or disperse the Lodge, which ought to be avoided by all that are true and faithful.

VII. Every new brother, at his entry, is decently to clothe the Lodge, that is, all the brethren present, and to deposit something for the relief of the indigent and decayed brethren, as the candidate shall see fit to bestow over and above the small allowance that may be stated in the by-laws of that particular Lodge, which charity shall be kept by the cashier; also, the candidate shall solemnly promise to submit to the Constitution, and other good usages that shall be intimated to him in time and place convenient.

VIII. No set or number of brethren shall withdraw or separate themselves from the Lodge in which they were made, or were afterwards admitted members, unless the Lodge become too numerous; nor even then, without a dispensation from the Grand Master or Deputy; and when thus separated, they must either immediately join themselves to such other Lodges that they shall like best, who are willing to receive them, or else obtain the Grand Master's Warrant to join in forming a new Lodge, to be regularly constituted in good time.

If any set or number of Masons shall take upon themselves to form a Lodge without the Grand Master's Warrant, the regular Lodges are not to countenance them, nor own them as fair brethren duly formed, nor approve of their acts and deeds; but must treat them as rebels, until they humble themselves as the Grand Master shall, in his prudence direct, and until he approve of them by his warrant signified to other Lodges, as the custom is when a new Lodge is to be registered in the Grand Lodge book.

IX. But if any brother so far misbehave himself as to render his Lodge uneasy, he shall be thrice duly admonished by the Master and Wardens in that Lodge formed; and if he will not refrain his imprudence, nor obediently submit to the advice of his brethren, he shall be dealt with according to the by-laws of that particular Lodge; or else in such a manner as the Grand Lodge shall in their great prudence think fit, for which a new regulation may be afterward made.

X. The majority of every particular Lodge, when congregated, not else, shall have the privilege of giving instructions to their Master and Wardens before the meeting of the Grand Lodge, because the said officers are their representatives, and supposed to speak the sentiments of their brethren at the said Grand Lodge.

XI. All particular Lodges are to observe the like usages as much as possible; in order to which, and also for cultivating a good understanding among Free-masons, some members of every Lodge should be deputed to visit other Lodges as often as shall be thought convenient.

XII. The Grand Lodge consists of, and is formed by, the Masters and Wardens of all the particular Lodges upon record, with the Grand Master at their head, the Deputy on his left hand, and the Grand Wardens in their places.

These must have their Quarterly Communications, or monthly meetings and adjournments, as often as occasion requires, in some convenient place, as the Grand Master shall appoint, where none shall be present but its own proper members, without leave asked and given; and while such a stranger, though a brother, stays, he is not allowed to vote, or even to speak on any question, without leave of the Grand Lodge, or unless he is desired to give his opinion.

All matters in the Grand Lodge are determined by

a majority of votes, each member having one vote, and the Grand Master two votes, unless the Grand Lodge leave any particular thing to the determination of the Grand Master for the sake of expedition.

XIII. At the Grand Lodge meetings, all matters that concern the Fraternity in general, or particular Lodges, or single brothers, are sedately and maturely to be discoursed of.

1. Apprentices must be admitted Fellow Crafts and Masters only here, unless by a dispensation from the Grand Master.

2. Here also all differences that cannot be made up or accommodated privately, nor by a particular Lodge, are to be seriously considered and decided; and if any brother thinks himself aggrieved by the decision, he may appeal to the Grand Lodge next ensuing, and leave his appeal in writing with the Grand Master, the Deputy, or Grand Wardens.

3. Hither also all the officers of particular Lodges shall bring a list of such members as have been made, or even admitted by them since the last Grand Lodge.

4. There shall be books kept by the Grand Master or Deputy, or rather by some other brother appointed Secretary of the Grand Lodge, wherein shall be recorded all the Lodges, with the usual times and places of their forming, and the names of all the members of each Lodge; also, all the affairs of the Grand Lodge that are proper to be written.

5. The Grand Lodge shall consider of the most

prudent and effectual means of collecting and disposing of what money shall be lodged with them on charity, towards the relief only of any true brother fallen into poverty and decay, but none else.

6. But each particular Lodge may dispose of their own charity for poor brothers, according to their own by-laws, until it be agreed by all the Lodges in a new regulation, to carry in the charity collected by them to the Grand Lodge at the Quarterly or Annual Communication, in order to make a common stock for the more handsome relief of poor brethren.

7. They shall appoint a Treasurer, a brother of worldly substance, who shall be a member of the Grand Lodge by virtue of his office, and shall be always present, and have power to move to the Grand Lodge any thing that concerns his office.

8. To him shall be committed all money raised for the general charity, or for any other use of the Grand Lodge, which he shall write down in a book, with the respective ends and uses for which the several sums are intended, and shall expend or disburse the same by such a certain order, signed as the Grand Lodge shall hereafter agree to in a new regulation.

But by virtue of his office, as Treasurer, without any other qualification, he shall not vote in choosing a new Grand Master and Grand Wardens, though in every other transaction.

9. In like manner the Secretary shall be a member of the Grand Lodge, by virtue of his office, and shall vote in every thing, except in choosing Grand Officers.

10. The Treasurer and Secretary may each have a Clerk or Assistant, if they think fit, who must be a brother and a Master Mason, but must never be a member of the Grand Lodge, nor speak without being allowed or commanded.

11. The Grand Master or Deputy have authority always to command the Treasurer and Secretary to attend him, with their Clerks and books, in order to see how matters go on, and to know what is expedient to be done upon an emergency.

12. Another brother and Master Mason should be appointed the Tyler, to look after the door; but he must be no member of the Grand Lodge.

13. But these offices may be further explained by a new regulation, when the necessity or expediency of them may more appear than at present to the Fraternity.

XIV. If at any Grand Lodge, stated or occasional, monthly or annual, the Grand Master and Deputy should both be absent, then the present Master of a Lodge that has been longest a Freemason, shall take the chair and preside as Grand Master, *pro tempore*, and shall be vested with all the honor and power for the time being, provided there is no brother present that has been Grand Master or Deputy formerly; for the last former Grand Master or Deputy in company takes place of right in the absence of a Grand Master or Deputy.

XV. In the Grand Lodge none can act as Wardens

but the present Grand Wardens, if in company; and, if absent, the Grand Master shall order private Wardens to act as Grand Wardens, *pro tempore*, whose places are to be supplied by two Fellow Crafts or Master Masons of the same Lodge, called forth to act, or sent thither by the Master thereof; or if by him omitted, the Grand Master, or he that presides, shall call them forth to act, so that the Grand Lodge may be always complete.

XVI. 1. The Grand Wardens or any others, are first to advise with the Deputy about the affairs of the Lodges of private single brothers, and are not to apply to the Grand Master without the knowledge of the Deputy, unless he refuse his concurrence.

2. In which case, or in case of any difference of sentiment between the Deputy and Grand Wardens, or other brothers, both parties are to go to the Grand Master by consent; who, by virtue of his great authority and power, can easily decide the controversy and make up the difference.

3. The Grand Master should not receive any private intimation of business concerning Masons and masonry, but from his Deputy first, except in such cases as his Worship can easily judge of; and if the application to the Grand Master be irregular, his Worship can order the Grand Wardens, or any so applying, to wait upon the Deputy, who is speedily to prepare the business and lay it orderly before his Worship.

XVII. No Grand Master, Grand Warden, Treasurer

or Secretary, or whoever acts for them, or in their stead, *pro tempore*, can, at the same time, act as the Master or Warden of a particular Lodge; but as soon as any of them has discharged his public office, he returns to that post or station in his particular Lodge from which he was called to officiate.

XVIII. 1. If the Deputy be sick, or necessarily absent, the Grand Master can choose any brother he pleases, to act as his Deputy, *pro tempore.*

2. But he that is chosen Deputy at the installation, and also the Grand Wardens, cannot be discharged, unless the cause fairly appear to the Grand Lodge.

3. For the Grand Master, if he is uneasy, may call a Grand Lodge on purpose to lay the case before them for their advice and concurrence.

And if the members of the Grand Lodge cannot reconcile the Grand Master with his Deputy or Wardens, they are to allow the Grand Master to discharge his Deputy or Wardens, and to choose another Deputy immediately; and the same Grand Lodge, in that case, shall forthwith choose other Grand Wardens, so that harmony and peace may be preserved.

XIX. If the Grand Master should abuse his great power, and render himself unworthy of the obedience and submission of the Lodge, he shall be treated in a way and manner to be agreed upon in a new regulation, because hitherto the ancient Fraternity have had no occasion for it.

XX. The Grand Master with his Deputy, Grand

Wardens, and Secretary, shall, at least once, go round and visit all the Lodges about town during his mastership.

XXI. If the Grand Master dies during his mastership, or by sickness, or by being beyond sea, or any other way be rendered incapable of discharging his office, the Deputy, or in his absence the Senior Grand Warden, or in his absence the Junior Grand Warden, or in his absence any three Masters of Lodges shall assemble the Grand Lodge immediately, in order to advise together upon the emergency, and to send two of their number to invite the last Grand Master to resume his office, which now of course reverts to him; and if he refuses to act, then the next last, and so backward; but if no former Grand Master be found, the present Deputy shall act as principal till a new Grand Master is chosen; or if there be no Deputy, then the oldest Mason, the present Master of a Lodge.

XXII. The brethren of all the regular Lodges in and near the city of London, shall meet in some convenient place on every St. John's day; and when business is over, they may repair to their festival dinners, as they shall think most convenient; and when St. John's day happen to be on a Sunday, then the public meeting shall be on the next Monday.

The Grand Lodge must meet in some convenient place on St. John the Evangelist's day, in every year, in order to proclaim the new or recognize the old Grand Master, Deputy, and Grand Wardens.

XXIII. If the present Grand Master shall consent to continue a second year, then one of the Grand Lodge deputed for that purpose, shall represent to all the brethren, his Worship's good government, &c., and turning to him, shall, in the name of the Grand Lodge, humbly request him to do the Fraternity the great honor, if nobly born, if not, the great kindness, of continuing to be their Grand Master for the year ensuing; and his Worship declaring his consent thereto, in manner he thinks proper, the Grand Secretary shall thrice proclaim him aloud—GRAND MASTER OF MASONS.

All the members of the Grand Lodge shall salute him in due form, according to the ancient and laudable customs of Freemasons.

XXIV. The present Grand Master shall nominate his successor for the year ensuing; who, if unanimously approved of by the Grand Lodge, and there present, he shall be proclaimed, saluted and congratulated, the new Grand Master as before hinted; and immediately be installed by the last Grand Master, according to an ancient usage.

But if that nomination is not unanimously approved, the new Grand Master shall be chosen immediately by ballot, viz.: every Master and Warden writing his man's name, and the last Grand Master writing his man's name too, and the man whose name the last Grand Master shall first take out casually, or by chance, shall be Grand Master of Masons for the year ensuing: and if present, he shall be proclaimed, saluted and congratulated, as before hinted, and forthwith installed by the last Grand Master, according to usage.

XXV. 1. The last Grand Master thus continued, or the new Grand Master thus installed, shall next, as his inherent right, nominate and appoint his Deputy Grand Master, either the last, or a new one, who shall also be proclaimed, saluted and congratulated, in due form.

2. The new Grand Master shall also nominate his new Grand Wardens; and, if unanimously approved by the Grand Lodge, they shall also be forthwith proclaimed, saluted and congratulated, in due form.

XXVI. That if any brother whom the present Grand Master shall nominate for his successsor, or whom the Grand Lodge shall choose by ballot, as above, be out of town, and has returned his answer that he will accept of the office of Grand Master, he shall be proclaimed, as before in regulation XXIII., and may be installed by proxy, which proxy must be the present or former Grand Master, who shall act in his name, and receive the usual honors, homage and congratulations.

XXVII. Every Grand Lodge has an inherent power and authority to make new regulations, or to alter those for the real benefit of the ancient fraternity, provided always, that the old landmarks be carefully preserved, and that such new regulations and alterations be proposed and agreed to by the Grand Lodge, and that they be submitted to the perusal of all the brethren, in writing, whose approbation and consent, or the majority thereof, is absolutely necessary to make the same binding and obligatory; which must, therefore, after the new Grand Master is installed, be solemnly desired and obtained from the Grand Lodge, as it was for these old regulations, by a great number of brethren.

Section Second.

REGULATIONS FOR THE GOVERNMENT OF THE GRAND LODGE, DURING THE TIME OF PUBLIC BUSINESS.

XXVIII. 1. That no brother be admitted into the Grand Lodge, but the immediate members thereof, viz: the four present and all former Grand Officers, the Treasurer, and Secretary, the Masters, Wardens, and Past Masters of all regular Lodges, except a brother who is a petitioner, or a witness in some case, or one called in by motion.

2. That at the third stroke of the Grand Master's gavel, there shall be a general silence; and that he who breaks silence, without leave from the chair, shall be publicly reprimanded.

3. That under the same penalty every brother shall keep his seat, and keep strict silence whenever the Grand Master or his Deputy shall think fit to rise from the chair, and call *to order*.

4. That in the Grand Lodge every member shall keep in his seat, (according to the number of his Lodge,) and not move about from place to place during the communication, except the Grand Wardens, as having more immediately the care of the Grand Lodge.

5. That no brother is to speak but once to the same

affair, unless to explain himself, or when called upon by the chair to speak.

6. Every one that speaks shall rise, and keep standing, addressing himself in a proper manner to the chair; nor shall any presume to interrupt him, under the aforesaid penalty; unless the Grand Master find him wandering from the point in hand, and shall think fit to reduce him to order; for then the said speaker shall sit down: but after he has been set right, he may again proceed, if he pleases.

7. If in the Grand Lodge any member is twice called to order at any one assembly, for transgressing these rules, and is guilty of a third offence of the same nature, the chair shall peremptorily order him to quit the Lodge room for that night.

8. That whoever shall be so rude as to hiss at any brother, or at what another says or has said, he shall be forthwith solemnly excluded the communication, and declared incapable of ever being a member of any Grand Lodge for the future, till another time he publicly owns his fault, and his grace be granted.

In order to preserve harmony, it was thought necessary to use counters and a ballotting box when occasion requires.

My son, forget not my law; but let thine heart keep my commandments, and remove not the ANCIENT LANDMARKS which thy fathers have set.—SOLOMON.

THE

CONSTITUTIONS OF THE FREE MASONS;

CONTAINING THE HISTORY, CHARGES, REGULATIONS, &C., OF THAT MOST ANCIENT AND RIGHT WORSHIPFUL FRATERNITY.

THE CHARGES OF A FREE MASON,

EXTRACTED from the ancient records of Lodges beyond sea, and of those in England, Scotland and Ireland, for the use of the Lodges in London: To be read at the making of new brethren, or when the Master shall order it.

THE GENERAL HEADS, VIZ:

I. Of God and Religion.
II. Of the Civil Magistrate, Supreme and Subordinate.
III. Of Lodges.
IV. Of Masters, Wardens, Fellows and Apprentices.
V. Of the Management of the Craft in Working.
VI. Of Behaviour, viz:

1. In the Lodge while constituted.

ANCIENT CONSTITUTIONS.

The following Constitutions are re-published from the first copy ever printed. At the Grand Lodge of England held on the 24th of June, 1721, the Duke of Montagu was elected Grand Master, who requested Dr. Desaguliers and James Anderson, D. D., "men of genius and education, to revise, arrange, and digest the Gothic Constitutions, old charges, and general regulations." This task they faithfully executed; and at the ensuing Grand Lodge held at the Queen's Arms, St. Paul's church yard, on the 27th of December 1721, being the festival of St. John the Evangelist, they presented the same for approbation. A committee of fourteen learned Brothers was then appointed to examine the manuscript, and to make their report; and on this occasion several very entertaining lectures were delivered, and much useful information given by a few old Brethren.

At a Grand Lodge held at the Fountain Tavern in the Strand in ample form on the 25th of March 1722, the committee reported that they had perused the manuscript containing the History, Charges, Regulations, &c., of masonry, and after some amendments had approved thereof. The Grand Lodge ordered the whole to be prepared for the press, and printed with all possible expedition. This order was strictly obeyed, and in little more than two years the Book of Constitutions appeared in print, under the following title: 'The Book of Constitutions of the Free Masons: Containing the History, Charges, Regulations, &c., of that most Ancient and Right Worshipful Fraternity. For the use of the Lodges.' London, 1723.

From that edition the following is re-published, for the purpose of placing it within the reach of every Mason, and preserving it for the craft in all coming time.

C. MOORE.

Cincinnati, Sept. 1850.

2. After the Lodge is over, and the Brethren not gone.

3. When Brethren meet without strangers, but not in a Lodge.

4. In presence of strangers not Masons.

5. At home, and in the neighberhood.

6. Towards a strange Brother.

I. CONCERNING GOD AND RELIGION.

A Mason is obliged, by his tenure, to obey the moral law; and if he rightly understands the art, he will never be a stupid atheist, nor an irreligious libertine. But though in ancient times Masons were charged in every country to be of the religion of that country or nation, whatever it was, yet 'tis now thought more expedient only to oblige them to that religion in which all men agree, leaving their particular opinions to themselves; that is, to be good men and true, or men of honor and honesty, by whatever denominations or persuasions they may be distinguished; whereby masonry becomes the center of union, and the means of conciliating true friendship among persons that must have remained at a perpetual distance.

II. OF THE CIVIL MAGISTRATE, SUPREME AND SUBORDINATE.

A Mason is to be a peaceable subject to the civil powers, wherever he resides or works, and is never to be concerned in plots and conspiracies against the peace and welfare of the nation, nor to behave himself undutifully to inferior magistrates; for as masonry hath been always injured by war, bloodshed, and confusion, so ancient kings and princes have been much disposed to encourage the craftsmen; because of their peaceableness and loyalty, whereby they practically answered the cavils of their adversaries, and promoted the honor of the fraternity, who ever flourished in times of peace. So that if a brother should be a rebel against the State, he is not to be countenanced in his rebellion, however he may be pitied as an unhappy man; and, if convicted of no other crime, though the loyal brotherhood must and ought to disown his rebellion, and give no umbrage or ground of political jealousy to the government for the time being, they cannot expel him from the Lodge, and his relation to it remains indefeasible.

III. OF LODGES.

A Lodge is a place where Masons assemble and work: Hence, that assembly, or duly organized society of Masons, is called a Lodge, and every brother ought to belong to one, and to be subject to its by-laws and general regulations. It is either particular or general, and will be best understood by attending it, and by the regulations of the General or Grand Lodge hereunto annexed. In ancient times, no Master or Fellow could be absent from it, especially when warned to appear at it, without incurring a severe censure, until it appeared to the Master and Wardens, that pure necessity hindered him.

The persons admitted members of a Lodge must be good and true men, free-born, and of mature and discreet age, no bondmen, no women, no immoral or scandalous men, but of good report.

VI. OF MASTERS, WARDENS, FELLOWS, AND APPRENTICES.

All preferment among Masons is grounded upon real worth and personal merit only; that so the lords may be well served, the brethren not put to shame, nor the Royal Craft despised: Therefore, no Master or Warden is chosen by seniority, but for his merit. It is impossible to describe these things in writing, and every brother must attend in his place, and learn them in a way peculiar to this fraternity: Only candidates may know, that no Master should take an Apprentice, unless he has sufficient employment for him, and unless he be a perfect youth, having no maim or defect in his body, that may render him incapable of learning the art, of serving his Master's lord, and of being made a brother, and then a Fellow Craft in due time, even after he has served such a term of years as the custom of the country directs; and that he should be descended of honest parents; that so, when otherwise qualified, he may arrive to the honor of being the Warden, and then the Master of the Lodge, the Grand Warden, and at length the Grand Master of all the Lodges, according to his merit.

No brother can be a Warden until he has passed the part of a Fellow Craft; nor a Master until he has acted as a Warden, nor Grand Warden until he has been Master of a Lodge, nor Grand Master unless he has been a Fellow Craft before his election, who is also to be nobly born, or a gentleman of the best fashion, or some eminent scholar, or some curious architect, or other artist, descended of honest parents, and who is of singular great merit in the opinion of the Lodges. And for the better and easier, and more honorable discharge of his office, the Grand Master has a power to choose his own Deputy Grand Master, who must be then, or must have been formerly, the Master of a particular Lodge, and has the privilege of acting whatever the Grand Master, his principal, should act, unless the said principal be present, or interpose his authority by a letter.

These rulers and governors, supreme and subordinate, of the Ancient Lodge, are to be obeyed in their respective stations by all the brethren, according to the old charges and regulations, with all humility, reverence, love and alacrity.

V. OF THE MANAGEMENT OF THE CRAFT IN WORKING.

All Masons shall work honestly on working days, that they may live creditably on holy days; and the time appointed by the law of the land or confirmed by custom, shall be observed.

The most expert of the Fellow Craftsmen shall be

appointed the Master, or Overseer of the lord's work; who is to be called Master by those that work under him. The Craftsmen are to avoid all ill language, and to call each other by no disobliging name, but brother or fellow; and to behave themselves courteously within and without the Lodge.

The Master, knowing himself to be able of cunning, shall undertake the lord's work as reasonably as possible, and truly dispend his goods as if they were his own; nor to give more wages to any brother or apprentice than he really may deserve.

Both the Master and the Masons, receiving their wages justly, shall be faithful to the lord, and honestly finish their work, whether task or journey; nor put the work to task, that hath been accustomed to journey.

None shall disvover envy at the prosperity of a brother, nor supplant him or put him out of his work, if he be capable to finish the same; for no man can finish another's work so much to the lord's profit, unless he be thoroughly acquainted with the designs and drafts of him that began it.

When a Fellow Craftsman is chosen Warden of the work under the Master, he shall be true both to Master and Fellows, shall carefully oversee the work in the Master's absence to the lord's profit; and his brethren shall obey him.

All Masons employed, shall meekly receive their wages, without murmuring or mutiny, and not desert the Master till the work is finished.

A younger brother shall be instructed in working, to prevent spoiling the materials for want of judgment, and for increasing and continuing of brotherly love.

All the tools used in working shall be approved by the Grand Lodge.

No laborer shall be employed in the proper work of masonry; nor shall Free Masons work with those that are not free, without an urgent necessity; nor shall they teach laborers and unaccepted Masons, as they should teach a brother or fellow.

VI. OF BEHAVIOUR, VIZ:

1. IN THE LODGE WHILE CONSTITUTED.

You are not to hold private committees, or separate conversation, without leave from the Master, nor to talk of any thing impertinent or unseemly, nor interrupt the Master or Wardens, or any brother speaking to the Master: Nor behave yourself ludicrously or jestingly while the Lodge is engaged in what is serious and solemn; nor use any unbecoming language upon any pretence whatsoever; but to pay due reverence to your Master, Wardens and Fellows, and put them to worship.

If any complaint be brought, the brother found guilty shall stand to the award and determination of the Lodge, who are the proper and competent judges of all such controversies, (unless you carry it by appeal to the Grand Lodge), and to whom they ought to be referred, unless a lord's work be hindered the mean while, in which case a particular reference may be made; but you must never go to law about what concerneth masonry, without an absolute necessity apparent to the Lodge.

2. BEHAVIOUR AFTER THE LODGE IS OVER, AND THE BRETHREN NOT GONE.

You may enjoy yourselves with innocent mirth, treating one another according to ability, but avoiding all excess, or forcing any brother to eat or drink beyond his inclination, or hindering him from going when his occasions call him, or doing or saying any thing offensive or that may forbid an easy and free conversation; for that would blast our harmony, and defeat our laudable purposes. Therefore, no private piques or quarrels must be brought within the door of the Lodge, far less any quarrels about religion, or nations, or State policy, we being only, as Masons, of the Catholic Religion above mentioned; we are also of all nations, tongues, kindreds, and languages, and are resolved against all politics, as what never yet conduced to the welfare of the Lodge, nor ever will. This charge has been always strictly enjoined and observed; but especially ever since the reformation in Britain, or the dissent and secession of these nations from the communion of Rome.

3. BEHAVIOUR WHEN BRETHREN MEET WITHOUT STRANGERS, BUT NOT IN A LODGE FORMED.

You are to salute one another in a courteous manner,

as you will be instructed, calling each other brother, freely giving mutual instruction, as shall be thought expedient, without being overseen or overheard, and without encroaching upon each other, or derogating from that respect which is due to any brother, were he not a Mason; for though all Masons are as brethren upon the same level, yet masonry takes no honor from a man that he had before; nay rather it adds to his honor, especially if he has deserved well of the brotherhood, who must give honor to whom it is due, and avoid ill manners.

4. BEHAVIOUR IN PRESENCE OF STRANGERS NOT MASONS.

You shall be cautious in your words and carriage, that the most penetrating stranger shall not be able to discover or find out what is not proper to be intimated; and sometimes you shall divert a discourse, and manage it prudently for the honor of the worshipful Fraternity.

5. BEHAVIOUR AT HOME AND IN YOUR NEIGHBORHOOD.

You are to act as becomes a moral and wise man; particularly, not to let your family, friends, and neighbors, know the concerns of the Lodge, &c., but wisely to consult your own honor, and that of the ancient brotherhood, for reasons not to be mentioned here. You must also consult your health, by not continuing together too late, or too long from home, after Lodge hours are past; and by avoiding of gluttony or drunkenness, that your families be not neglected or injured, nor you disabled from working.

6. BEHAVIOUR TOWARDS A STRANGE BROTHER.

You are cautiously to examine him, in such a method as prudence shall direct you, that you may not be imposed upon by an ignorant false pretender, whom you are to reject with contempt and derision, and beware of giving him any hints of knowledge.

But if you discover him to be a true and genuine brother, you are to respect him accordingly; and if he is in want, you must relieve him if you can, or else direct him how he may be relieved: You must employ him some days, or else recommend him to be employed. But you are not charged to do beyond your ability, only to prefer a poor brother, that is a good man and true, before any other poor people in the same circumstances.

Finally, All these charges you are to observe, and also those that are to be communicated to you in another way; cultivating *brotherly love,* the foundation and cap-stone, the cement and glory of this ancient fraternity, avoiding all wrangling and quarrelling, all slander and backbiting, nor permitting others to slander any honest brother, but defending his character, and doing him all good offices, as far as is consistent with your honor and safety, and no farther. And if any of them do you injury, you must apply to your own or his Lodge; and from thence you may appeal to the Grand Lodge at the quarterly communication, and from thence to the annual Grand Lodge, as has been the ancient laudable conduct of our forefathers in every nation; never taking a legal course but when the case cannot be otherwise decided, and patiently listening to the honest and friendly advice of Master and Fellows, when they would prevent your going to law with strangers, or would excite you to put a speedy period to all law suits, that so you may mind the affair of masonry with the more alacrity and success; but with respect to brothers or fellows at law, the Master and brethren should kindly offer their mediation, which ought to be thankfully submitted to by the contending brethren; and if that submission is impracticable, they must however, carry on their process, or law suit, without wrath and rancor, (not in the common way,) saying or doing nothing which may hinder brotherly love, and good offices to be renewed and continued; that all may see the benign influence of masonry, as all true Masons have done from the beginning of the world, and will do to the end of time. Amen, so mote it be.

POSTSCRIPT.

A worthy brother, learned in the law, has communicated to the Author (while this sheet was printing) the opinion of the great Judge Coke upon the act against Masons, 3 Hen. VI. Chap. 1. which is printed in this Book, page, 35, and which quotation the Author has compared with the original, viz:

COKE'S INSTITUTES, 3D PART, FOL. 99.

The cause wherefore this offence was made felony, is for that the good course and effect of the statutes of laborers were thereby violated and broken. Now, (says my Lord Coke) all the statutes concerning laborers, before this act, and whereunto this act doth refer, are repealed by the statute of 5. *Eliz. Cap.* 4. whereby the cause and end of the making of this act, is taken away; and consequently this act is become of no force or effect: for *cessante ratione Legis, cessat ipsa Lex:* And the indictment of felony upon this statute must contain, that those Chapters and Congregations were to the violating and breaking of the good course and effect of the statutes of laborers; which now cannot be so alleged, because the statutes be repealed. Therefore, this would be put out of the charge of justices of peace, written by Master Lambert, p. 227.

This quotation confirms the tradition of old Masons, that this most learned Judge really belonged to the ancient Lodge, and was a faithful brother.

GENERAL REGULATIONS,

Compiled first by Mr. George Payne, *Anno*, 1720, when he was Grand Master, and approved by the Grand Lodge on St. John Baptist's Day, *Anno*, 1721, at Stationer's Hall, London; when the most noble prince, JOHN, DUKE OF MONTAGU, was unanimously chosen our Grand Master for the year ensuing; who chose JOHN BEAL, M. D. his Deputy Grand Master; Mr. JOSIAH VILLINEAU, and Mr. THOMAS MORRIS, Jr. were chosen by the Lodge Grand Wardens. And now, by the command of our said Right Worshipful Grand Master MONTAGU, the Author of this Book has compared them with, and reduced them to the ancient records and immemorial usages of the Fraternity, and digested them into this new method, with several proper explications, for the use of the Lodges in and about London and Westminster.

I. The Grand Master, or his Deputy, hath authority and right, not only to be present in any true Lodge, but also to preside wherever he is, with the Master of the Lodge on his left hand, and to order his Grand Wardens to attend him, who are not to act in particular Lodges as Wardens, but in his presence, and at his command; because there the Grand Master may command the Wardens of that Lodge, or any other brethren, he pleaseth, to attend and act as his Wardens *pro tempore.*

II. The Master of a particular Lodge has the right and authority of congregating the members of his Lodge into a Chapter at pleasure, upon any emergency or occurrence, as well as to appoint the time and place of their usual forming: And in case of sickness, death, or necessary absence of the Master, the Senior Warden shall act as Master *pro tempore*, if no brother is present who has been Master of that Lodge before; for in that case, the absent Master's authority reverts to the last Master then present, though he cannot act until the said Senior Warden has once congregated the Lodge, or in his absence the Junior Warden.

III. The Master of each particular Lodge, or one of the Wardens, or some other brother by his order, shall keep a book containing their by-laws, the names of their members, with a list of all the Lodges in town, and the usual times and places of their forming, and all their transactions that are proper to be written.

IV. No Lodge shall make more than five new brethren at one time, nor any man under the age of twenty-five, who must be also his own master; unless by a dispensation from the Grand Master or his Deputy.

V. No man can be made or admitted a member of a particular Lodge, without previous notice, one month before given to the said Lodge, in order to make due enquiry into the reputation and capacity of the candidate; unless by the dispensation aforesaid.

VI. But no man can be entered a Brother in any particular Lodge, or admitted to be a member thereof, without the unanimous consent of all the members of that Lodge then present, when the candidate is proposed, and their consent is formally asked by the Master; and they are to signify their consent or dissent in their own prudent way, either virtually or in form, but with unanimity; nor is this inherent privilege subject to a dispensation; because the members of a particular Lodge are the best judges of it; and if a fractious member should be imposed on them, it might spoil their harmony, or hinder their freedom: or even break and disperse the Lodge, which ought to be avoided by all good and true brethren.

VII. Every new brother at his making is decently to clothe the Lodge, that is, all the brethren present, and to deposit something for the relief of the indigent and decayed brethren, as the candidate shall think fit to bestow, over and above the small allowance stated by the by-laws of that particular Lodge: which charity shall be lodged with the Master or Wardens, or the cashier, if the members think fit to choose one.

And the candidate shall also solemnly promise to submit to the Constitutions, the Charges, and Regulations, and to such other good usages as shall be intimated to them in time and place convenient.

VIII. No set or number of brethren shall withdraw or separate themselves from the Lodge in which they were made brethren, or were afterwards admitted members, unless the Lodge becomes too numerous, nor even then, without a dispensation from the Grand

Master or his Deputy: And when they are thus separated, they must either immediately join themselves to such other Lodge as they shall like best, with the unanimous consent of that other Lodge to which they go (as above regulated) or else they must obtain the Grand Master's warrant to join in forming a new Lodge.

If any set or number of Masons shall take upon themselves to form a Lodge without the Grand Master's warrant, the regular Lodges are not to countenance them, nor own them as fair brethren and duly formed, nor approve of their acts and deeds; but must treat them as rebels, until they humble themselves, as the Grand Master shall, in his prudence direct, and until he approve of them by his warrant, which must be signified to the other Lodges, as the custom is when a new Lodge is to be registered in the list of Lodges.

IX. But if any brother so far misbehave himself as to render his Lodge uneasy, he shall be twice duly admonished by the Master or Wardens in a formed Lodge; and if he will not refrain his imprudence, and obediently submit to the advice of the brethren, and reform what gives them offence, he shall be dealt with according to the by-laws of that particular Lodge, or else in such a manner as the Quarterly Communication shall in their great prudence think fit; for which a new regulation may be afterwards made.

X. The majority of every particular Lodge, when congregated, shall have the privilege of giving instructions to their Master and Wardens, before the assembling of the Grand Chapter, or Lodge, at the three Quarterly Communications hereafter mentioned, and of the Annual Grand Lodge too; because their Master and Wardens are their representatives, and are supposed to speak their mind.

XI. All particular Lodges are to observe the same usages as much as possible; in order to which, and for cultivating a good understanding among Free Masons, some members out of every Lodge shall be deputed to visit the other Lodges as often as shall be thought convenient.

XII. The Grand Lodge consists of, and is formed by the Masters and Wardens of all the regular particular Lodges upon record, with the Grand Master at their head, and his Deputy on his left hand, and the Grand Wardens in their proper places; and must have a Quarterly Communication about Michaelmas, Christmas, and Lady-Day, in some convenient place, as the Grand Master shall appoint, where no brother shall be present, who is not at that time a member thereof, without a dispensation; and while he stays, he shall not be allowed to vote, nor even give his opinion, without leave of the Grand Lodge, asked and given, or unless it be duly asked by the said Lodge.

All matters are to be determined in the Grand Lodge by a majority of votes, each member having one vote, and the Grand Master having two votes, unless the said Lodge leave any particular thing to the determination of the Grand Master, for the sake of expedition.

XIII. At the said Quarterly Communication, all matters that concern the Fraternity in general, or particular Lodges, or single brethren, are quietly, sedately, and maturely to be discoursed of and transacted: Apprentices must be admitted Masters and Fellow Craft only here, unless by a dispensation. Here also all differences, that cannot be made up and accommodated privately, nor by a particular Lodge, are to be seriously considered and decided. And if any brother thinks himself aggrieved by the decision of this board, he may appeal to the Annual Grand Lodge next ensuing, and leave his appeal in writing, with the Grand Master, or his Deputy, or the Grand Wardens.

Here also, the Master or the Wardens of each particular Lodge, shall bring and produce a list of such members as have been made, or even admitted in their particular Lodges, since the last communication of the Grand Lodge: And there shall be a book kept by the Grand Master, or his Deputy, or rather by some brother whom the Grand Lodge shall appoint for Secretary, wherein shall be recorded all the Lodges, with their usual times and places of forming, and names of all the members of each Lodge; and all the affairs of the Grand Lodge that are proper to be written.

They shall also consider of the most prudent and effectual methods of collecting and disposing of what money shall be given to, or lodged with them in charity, towards the relief only of any true brother, fallen into poverty or decay, but of none else: But every particular

Lodge shall dispose of their own charity for poor brethren, according to their own by-laws, until it be agreed by all the Lodges (in a new regulation) to carry in the charity collected by them to the Grand Lodge at the Quarterly or Annual Communication, in order to make a common stock of it, for the more handsome relief of poor brethren.

They shall also appoint a Treasurer, a brother of good worldly substance, who shall be a member of the Grand Lodge by virtue of his office, and shall be always present, and have power to move to the Grand Lodge any thing, especially what concerns his office. To him shall be committed all money raised for charity, or for any other use of the Grand Lodge, which he shall write down in a book, with the respective ends and uses for which the several sums are intended; and shall expend or disburse the same by such a certain order signed, as the Grand Lodge shall afterwards agree to in a new regulation: But he shall not vote in choosing a Grand Master or Wardens, though in every other transaction. As in like manner the Secretary shall be a member of the Grand Lodge by virtue of his office, and vote in every thing except in choosing a Grand Master or Wardens.

The Treasurer and Secretary shall have each a clerk, who must be a brother and Fellow Craft, but never must be a member of the Grand Lodge, nor speak without being allowed or desired.

The Grand Master, or his Deputy, shall always

command the Treasurer and Secretary, with their clerks and books, in order to see how matters go on, and to know what is expedient to be done upon any emergent occasion.

Another brother (who must be a Fellow Craft) should be appointed to look after the door of the Grand Lodge; but shall be no member of it.

But these offices may be farther explained by a new regulation, when the necessity and expediency of them may more appear than at present to the Fraternity.

XIV. If at any Grand Lodge, stated or occasional, quarterly or annual, the Grand Master and his Deputy should be both absent, then the present Master of a Lodge, that has been the longest a Free Mason, shall take the chair, and preside as Grand Master *pro tempore;* and shall be vested with all his power and honor for the time; provided there is no brother present that has been Grand Master formerly, or Deputy Grand Master; for the last Grand Master present, or else the last Deputy present, should always of right, take place in the absence of the present Grand Master and his Deputy.

XV. In the Grand Lodge none can act as Wardens but the Grand Wardens themselves, if present; and if absent, the Grand Master, or the person who presides in his place, shall order private Wardens to act as Grand Wardens *pro tempore*, whose places are to be supplied by two Fellow Craft of the same Lodge, called forth to act, or sent thither by the particular Master thereof;

or if by him omitted, then they shall be called by the Grand Master, that so the Grand Lodge may be always complete.

XVI. The Grand Wardens or any others, are first to advise with the Deputy about the affairs of the Lodge or of the brethren, and not to apply to the Grand Master without the knowledge of the Deputy, unless he refuse his concurrence in any certain necessary affair; in which case, or in case of any difference between the Deputy and the Grand Wardens, or other brethren, both parties are to go by concert to the Grand Master, who can easily decide the controversy, and make up the difference by virtue of his great authority.

The Grand Master should receive no intimation of business concerning masonry, but from his Deputy first, except in such certain cases as his Worship can well judge of; for if the application to the Grand Master be irregular, he can easily order the Grand Wardens, or any other brethren thus applying, to wait upon his Deputy, who is to prepare the business speedily, and to lay it orderly before his Worship.

XVII. No Grand Master, Deputy Grand Master, Grand Wardens, Treasurer, Secretary, or whoever acts for them, or in their stead, *pro tempore,* can at the same time be the Master or Warden of a particular Lodge; but as soon as any of them has honorably discharged his Grand Office, he returns to that post or station in his particular Lodge, from which he was called to officiate above.

XVIII. If the Deputy Grand Master be sick, or necessarily absent, the Grand Master may choose any Fellow Craft he pleases, to be his Deputy *pro tempore:* But he that is chosen Deputy at the Grand Lodge, and the Grand Wardens too, cannot be discharged without the cause fairly appear to the majority of the Grand Lodge; and the Grand Master if he is uneasy, may call a Grand Lodge on purpose to lay the cause before them, and to have their advice and concurrence: In which case, the majority of the Grand Lodge, if they cannot reconcile the Master and his Deputy or his Wardens, are to concur in allowing the Master to discharge his said Deputy or his said Wardens, and to choose another Deputy immediately; and the said Grand Lodge shall choose other Wardens in that case, that harmony and peace may be preserved.

XIX. If the Grand Master should abuse his power, and render himself unworthy of the obedience and subjection of the Lodge, he shall be treated in a way and manner to be agreed upon in a new regulation; because hitherto the ancient Fraternity have had no occasion for it, their former Grand Masters having all behaved themselves worthy of that honorable office.

XX. The Grand Master with his Deputy and Wardens, shall (at least once) go round and visit all the Lodges about town during his Mastership.

XXI. If the Grand Master die during his Mastership, or by sickness, or by being beyond sea, or any other way should be rendered uncapable of discharging his office, the Deputy, or in his absence the Senior Grand Warden, or in his absence the Junior, or in his absence any three present Masters of Lodges, shall join to congregate the Grand Lodge immediately, to advise together upon that emergency, and to send two of their number to invite the last Grand Master to resume his office, which now in course reverts to him; or if he refuse, then the next last, and so backward: But if no former Grand Master can be found, then the Deputy shall act as principal, until another is chosen; or if there be no deputy, then the oldest Master.

XXII. The brethren of all the Lodges in and about London and Westminster, shall meet at an Annual Communication and Feast, in some convenient place, on St. John Baptist's day, or else on St. John Evangelist's day, as the Grand Lodge shall think fit by a new regulation, having of late years met on St. John Baptist's day: *Provided,* the majority of the Masters and Wardens, with the Grand Master, his Deputy and Wardens, agree at their Quarterly Communication, three months before, that there shall be a feast, and a General Communication of all the brethren: For, if either the Grand Master, or the majority of the particular Masters, are against it, it must be dropt for that time.

But whether there shall be a feast for all the brethren, or not, yet the Grand Lodge must meet in some convenient place annually on St. John's day; or if it be Sunday, then on the next day, in order to choose every year a new Grand Master, Deputy, and Wardens.

XXIII. If it be thought expedient, and the Grand Master, with the majority of the Masters and Wardens, agree to hold a Grand Feast, according to the ancient laudable custom of Masons, then the Grand Wardens shall have the care of preparing the tickets, sealed with the Grand Master's seal, of disposing of the tickets, of receiving the money for the tickets, of buying the materials of the feast, of finding out a proper and convenient place to feast in, and of every other thing that concerns the entertainment.

But that the work may not be too burthensome to the two Grand Wardens, and that all matters may be expeditiously and safely managed, the Grand Master, or his Deputy shall have power to nominate and appoint a certain number of Stewards, as his Worship shall think fit, to act in concert with the two Grand Wardens; all things relating to the feast being decided amongst them by a majority of voices; except the Grand Master or his Deputy interpose by a particular direction or appointment.

XXIV. The Wardens and Stewards shall, in due time, wait upon the Grand Master, or his Deputy, for directions and orders about the premises; but if his Worship and his Deputy are sick, or necessarily absent, they shall call together the Masters and Wardens of Lodges to meet on purpose for their advice and orders; or else they may take the matter wholly upon themselves, and do the best they can.

The Grand Wardens and the Stewards are to account

for all the money they receive, or expend, to the Grand Lodge, after dinner, or when the Grand Lodge shall think fit to receive their accounts.

If the Grand Master pleases, he may in due time summon all the Masters and Wardens of Lodges to consult with them about ordering the Grand Feast, and about any emergency or accidental thing relating thereunto, that may require advice; or else to take it upon himself altogether.

XXV. The Masters of Lodges shall each appoint one experienced and discreet Fellow Craft of his Lodge, to compose a committee, consisting of one from every Lodge, who shall meet to receive, in a convenient appartment, every person that brings a ticket, and shall have power to discourse him, if they think fit, in order to admit him, or debar him, as they shall see cause. *Provided*, they send no man away before they have acquainted all the brethren within the doors with the reason thereof, to avoid mistakes; that so no true brother may be debarred, nor a false brother, or mere pretender admitted. This committee must meet very early on St. John's day at the place, even before any persons come with tickets.

XXVI. The Grand Master shall appoint two or more trusty brethren to be porters, or door-keepers, who are also to be early at the place, for some good reasons; and who are to be at the command of the committee.

XXVII. The Grand Wardens, or the Stewards, shall appoint beforehand such a number of brethren to serve at table as they think fit and proper for that work; and they may advise with the Masters and Wardens of Lodges about the most proper persons, if they please, or may take in such by their recommendation; for none are to serve that day, but free and accepted Masons, that the Communication may be free and harmonious.

XXVIII. All the members of the Grand Lodge must be at the place long before dinner, with the Grand Master, or his Deputy, at their head, who shall retire, and form themselves. And this is done in order,

1. To receive any appeals duly lodged, as above regulated, that the appellant may be heard, and the affair may be amicably decided before dinner, if possible; but if it cannot, it must be delayed till after the new Grand Master is elected; and if it cannot be decided after dinner, it may be delayed, referred to a particular committee, that shall quietly adjust it, and make report to the next Quarterly Communication, that brotherly love may be preserved.

2. To prevent any difference or disgust which may be feared to arise that day; that no interruption may be given to the harmony and pleasure of the Grand Feast.

3. To consult about whatever concerns the decency and decorum of the Grand Asssembly, and to prevent all indecency and ill manners, the assembly being promiscuous.

4. To receive and consider of any good motion, or any momentous and important affair, that shall be

brought from the particular Lodges, by their Representatives, the several Masters and Wardens.

XXIX. After these things are discussed, the Grand Master and his Deputy, the Grand Wardens, or the Stewards, the Secretary, the Treasurer, the Clerks, and every other person, shall withdraw, and leave the Masters and Wardens of the particular Lodges alone, in order to consult amicably about electing a new Grand Master, or continuing the present, if they have not done it the day before: and if they are unanimous for continuing the present Grand Master, his Worship shall be called in, and humbly desired to do the fraternity the honor of ruling them for the year ensuing: and after dinner it will be known whether he accepts of it or not: for it should not be discovered but by the election itself.

XXX. Then the Masters and Wardens, and all the brethren, may converse promiscuously, or as they please to sort together, until the dinner is coming in, when every brother takes his seat at table.

XXXI. Some time after dinner the Grand Lodge is formed, not in retirement, but in the presence of all the brethren, who yet are not members of it, and must not speak until they are desired and allowed.

XXXII. If the Grand Master of last year has consented with the Master and Wardens in private, before dinner, to continue for the year ensuing, then one of the Grand Lodge, deputed for that purpose, shall represent to all the brethren his Worship's good government, &c. And turning to him, shall, in the name of the Grand Lodge, humbly request him to do the fraternity the great honor (if nobly born, if not) the great kindness, of continuing to be their Grand Master for the year ensuing. And his Worship declaring his consent by a bow or speech, as he pleases, the said deputed member of the Grand Lodge shall proclaim him Grand Master, and all the members of the Lodge shall salute him in due form. And all the brethren shall for a few minutes have leave to declare their satisfaction, pleasure and congratulation.

XXXIII. But if either the Master and Wardens have not in private, this day before dinner, nor the day before, desired the last Grand Master to continue in the Mastership another year; or if he, when desired, has not consented: then, the last Grand Master shall nominate his successor for the year ensuing, who, if unanimously approved by the Grand Lodge, and if there present, shall be proclaimed, saluted, and congratulated the new Grand Master as above hinted, and immediately installed by the last Grand Master, according to usage.

XXXIV. But, if that nomination is not unanimously approved, the new Grand Master shall be chosen immediately by ballot, every Master and Warden writing his man's name, and the last Grand Master writing his man's name too; and the man, whose name the last Grand Master shall first take out, casually or by chance, shall be Grand Master for the year ensuing; and if present, he shall be proclaimed, saluted, and congratulated, as above hinted, and forthwith installed by the last Grand Master, according to usage.

XXXV. The last Grand Master thus continued, or the new Grand Master thus installed, shall next nominate and appoint his Deputy Grand Master, either the last or a new one, who shall be also declared, saluted and congratulated as above hinted.

The Grand Master shall also nominate the new Grand Wardens, and if unanimously approved by the Grand Lodge, shall be declared, saluted, and congratulated, as above hinted; but if not, they shall be chosen by ballot, in the same way as the Grand Master: As the Wardens of private Lodges are also to be chosen by ballot in each Lodge, if the members thereof do not agree to their Master's nomination.

XXXVI. But if the brother whom the present Grand Master shall nominate for his successor, or whom the majority of the Grand Lodge shall happen to choose by ballot, is, by sickness or other necessary occasion, absent from the Grand Feast, he cannot be proclaimed the new Grand Master, unless the old Grand Master, or some of the Masters and Wardens of the Grand Lodge can vouch, upon the honor of a brother, that the said person, so nominated or chosen, will readily accept of the said office; in which case the old Grand Master shall act as proxy, and shall nominate the Deputy and Wardens in his name, and in his name also receive the usual honors, homage and congratulations.

XXXVII. Then the Grand Master shall allow any

brother, Fellow Craft, or Apprentice, to speak, directing his discourse to his Worship; or to make any motion for the good of the fraternity, which shall be either immediately considered and finished, or else referred to the consideration of the Grand Lodge at their next communication, stated or occasional. When that is over,

XXXVIII. The Grand Master or his Deputy, or some brother appointed by him, shall harangue all the brethren, and give them good advice: And lastly, after some other transactions, that cannot be written in any language, the brethren may go away or stay longer, as they please.

XXXIX. Every annual Grand Lodge has an inherent power and authority to make new regulations or to alter these, for the real benefit of this ancient fraternity: *Provided always*, that the old land-marks be carefully preserved, and that such alterations and new regulations be proposed and agreed to at the third Quarterly Communication preceding the annual Grand Feast; and that they be offered also to the perusal of all the brethren before dinner, in writing, even of the youngest apprentice; the approbation and consent of the majority of all the brethren present being absolutely necessary to make the same binding and obligatory; which must after dinner, and after the new Grand Master is installed, be solemnly desired; as it was desired and obtained for these regulations, when proposed by the Grand Lodge, to about one hundred and fifty brethren, on St. John Baptist's day, seventeen hundred and twenty-one.

POSTSCRIPT.

Here follows the manner of constituting a new Lodge, as practiced by his grace, the *Duke of Wharton.* the present Right Worshipful Grand Master, according to the ancient usages of Masons.

A new Lodge, for avoiding many irregularities, should be solemnly constituted by the Grand Master, with his Deputy and Wardens; or in the Grand Master's absence, the Deputy shall act for his Worship, and shall choose some Master of a Lodge to assist him; or in case the Deputy is absent, the Grand Master shall call forth some Master of a Lodge to act as Deputy *pro tempore.*

The candidates, or the new Master and Wardens, being yet among the Fellow Craft, the Grand Master shall ask his Deputy if he has examined them, and finds the candidate Master well skilled in the noble science and the royal art, and duly instructed in our mysteries, &c.

And the Deputy answering in the affirmative, he shall (by the Grand Master's order) take the candidate from among his fellows, and present him to the Grand Master; saying, Right Worshipful Grand Master, the brethren here desire to be formed into a new Lodge; and I present this my worthy brother to be their Master, whom I know to be of good morals and great skill, true and trusty, and a lover of the whole fraternity, wheresoever dispersed over the face of the earth.

Then the Grand Master, placing the candidate on his left hand, having asked and obtained the unanimous consent of all the brethren, shall say: I constitute and form these good brethren into a new Lodge, and appoint you the Master of it, not doubting of your capacity and care to preserve the cement of the Lodge, &c., with some other expressions that are proper and usual on that occasion; but not proper to be written.

Upon this the Deputy shall rehearse the charges of a Master, and the Grand Master shall ask the candidate, saying, Do you submit to these charges as Masters have done in all ages? And the candidate signifying his cordial submission thereunto, the Grand Master shall, by certain significant ceremonies and ancient usages, instal him, and present him with the Constitutions, the Lodge Book, and the instruments of his office, not altogether, but one after another; and after each of them, the Grand Master, or his Deputy, shall rehearse the short and pithy charge that is suitable to the thing presented.

After this, the members of this new Lodge, bowing all together to the Grand Master, shall return his Worship thanks, and immediately do their homage to their new Master, and signify their promise of subjection and obedience to him by the usual congratulation.

The Deputy and the Grand Wardens, and any other brethren present, that are not members of this new

Lodge, shall next congratulate the new Master; and he shall return his becoming acknowledgments to the Grand Master first, and to the rest in their order.

Then the Grand Master desires the new Master to enter immediately upon the exercise of his office, in choosing his Wardens; and the new Master calling forth two Fellow Craft, presents them to the Grand Master for his approbation, and to the new Lodge for their consent. And that being granted,

The Senior or Junior Grand Wardens, or some brother for him, shall rehearse the charges of Wardens; and the candidates being solemnly asked by the new Master, shall signify their submission thereunto.

Upon which the new Master, presenting them with the instruments of their office, shall, in due form, instal them in their proper places: and the brethren of that new Lodge shall signify their obedience to the new Wardens by the usual congratulation.

And this Lodge being thus completely constituted, shall be registered in the Grand Master's Book, and by his order notified to the other Lodges.

APPROBATION.

WHEREAS, by the confusions occasioned in the Saxon, Danish and Norman wars, the records of Masons have been much vitiated, the Free Masons of England twice thought it necessary to correct their Constitutions, Charges, and Regulations; first in the reign of King Athelstan, the Saxon, and long after in the reign of King Edward IV. the Norman: And, whereas, the old Constitutions in England have been much interpolated, mangled and miserably corrupted, not only with false spelling, but even with many false facts and gross errors in history and chronology, through length of time, and the ignorance of transcribers, in the dark illiterate ages, before the revival of geometry and ancient architecture, to the great offence of all the learned and judicious brethren, whereby also the ignorant have been deceived.

And our late Worthy Grand Master, his grace, the Duke of Montagu, having ordered the author to peruse, correct and digest, into a new and better method, the history, charges and regulations, of the ancient fraternity; he has accordingly examined several copies from Italy and Scotland, and sundry parts of England and from thence, (though in many things erroneous) and from several other ancient records of Masons, he has drawn forth the above written new Constitutions, with the Charges and General Regulations. And the author having submitted the whole to the perusal and corrections of the late and present Deputy Grand Masters, and of other learned brethren; and also of the Masters and Wardens of particular Lodges at their Quarterly Communication: he did regularly deliver them to the late Grand Master himself, the said Duke of Montagu, for his examination, correction, and approbation; and his grace, by the advice of several brethren, ordered the same to be handsomely printed for the use of the Lodges, though they were not quite ready for the press during his Mastership.

Therefore, we, the present Grand Master of the Right Worshipful and most ancient Fraternity of Free and Accepted Masons, the Deputy Grand Master, the Grand Wardens, the Masters and Wardens of particular Lodges (with the consent of the brethren and fellows in and about the cities of London and Westminster) having also perused this performance, do join our laudable predecessors in our *solemn approbation* thereof, as what we believe will fully answer the end proposed; all the valuable things of the old records being retained, the errors in history and chronology corrected, the false facts and the improper words omitted, and the whole digested in a new and better method,

And we ordain, that these be received in every particular Lodge under our cognizance, as the *only Constitutions* of Free and Accepted Masons amongst us, to be read at the making of new brethren, or when the Master shall think fit; and which the new brethren should peruse before they are made.

PHILIP, DUKE OF WHARTON,
Grand Master.

J. T. DESAGULIERS, LL. D. AND F. R. S.
Deputy Grand Master.

JOSHUA TIMSON,
WILLIAM HAWKINS, } *Wardens.*

FORM FOR A DISPENSATION.

TO ALL THE FRATERNITY:

The M. W. GRAND LODGE OF FREE AND ACCEPTED MASONS *of the State of* ——— *sends Greeting:*

WHEREAS, a petition has been presented to the undersigned, —— ———, Grand Master of the Grand Lodge of the State of ———, by Brothers A. B., C. D., E. F., &c., all Free and Accepted Ancient MASTER MASONS, praying to be congregated into a regular Lodge by the name of ——— Lodge, in the —— of ———, county of ——— and State of ———: And whereas said petitioners have been duly recommended to me and vouched for as MASTER MASONS in good standing by ——— Lodge, No. —, under our jurisdiction; and said application being in all respects in conformity with the requirements of the Constitution and By-laws of the Grand Lodge:—

NOW, THEREFORE BE IT KNOWN, That I, ———, Grand Master of the Grand Lodge of Free and Accepted Ancient York Masons of the State of ———, reposing full confidence in the recommendation aforesaid, and in the integrity and attachment of the aforesaid Petitioners to the sublime principles of MASONRY as originally taught and by us recognized: And believing that the interests of masonry will be promoted by granting the prayer of said petitioners, have granted, and do by the authority in me vested, hereby grant this my LETTER OF DISPENSATION, constituting the said Petitioners, and such others as they may masonically associate with them for that purpose, a regular and constitutional LODGE OF ANCIENT YORK MASONS, by the name and style of ——— Lodge. And I do hereby appoint Brother —— ——— to be the first Master;

Brother —— ——— to be first Senior Warden; and Brother —— ——— to be the first Junior Warden; hereby granting unto them full power and authority to assemble together on all proper and lawful occasions, as a LEGAL LODGE in the ——— of ———, county and State aforesaid; and when so assembled, to confer the several degrees of *Entered Apprentice, Fellow Craft,* and *Master Mason,* upon all such good men and true as may make application, according to the ancient custom, and not otherwise: and do all such other acts as a legal Lodge under Dispensation may of right do. And I hereby enjoin upon said Lodge, in all its acts, a strict conformity to the requirements of the Constitution, By-laws, Rules and Regulations of the Grand Lodge; requiring of them to be present by their Representatives or proxy, at the next ensuing Annual Communication of the Grand Lodge, and have there this Letter of Dispensation, together with a copy of the By-laws of their Lodge, and record of their proceedings, for the inspection of the Grand Lodge:—at which time the powers and privileges hereby granted shall cease.

IN TESTIMONY WHEREOF, I have hereunto subscribed my name, and affixed my private seal, at —— this ——— day of ———, A. L. 58—, A. D. 18—.

SEAL.

—— ———, *Grand Master.*

CHARGE TO A GRAND MASTER AT HIS INSTALLATION.

Let me congratulate you, Right Worshipful Sir, on the honor of being raised, from the level of equality, to the high station of presiding over all the Lodges of the State of ———, and the masonic jurisdiction thereof. We look up with confidence to a brother whose person is endeared to us by that love of the fraternity which is sanctified by the experience of many revolving years. May the Father of light, of life and of love, invest you with his choicest gifts—may heavenly wisdom illumine your mind—may heavenly power give strength to your exertions—may heavenly goodness fill and enlarge your breast—may your feet rest upon the rock of justice—from your hands may streams of beneficence continually flow: And round your head may there bend a circle made splendid by the rays of honor: And late, very late in life, may you be transmitted from the fading honor of an earthly Lodge, to the mansions prepared for the faithful in another and a better world.

Let me congratulate you, Right Worshipful Grand Officers and other brethren, on the election of our Grand Master; as it is *his,* agreeably to the rules of our institution, to *command,* so it is *ours* with readiness to *obey.* Look to the Sun and behold the planetary worlds revolving round him in continual order with the happiest effect, and learn to imitate their regularity, in hope of obtaining from the chair of *Solomon* the light of wisdom and the warmth of love. Or look higher still and behold the angels, those sister spirits Cherubim and Seraphim, who are exhibited to us in the oracles of revelation, as flaming spirits, burning with the heat in their heavenly Grand Master's service, and with love to his person and to each other; they are styled ministering spirits, from the part they take in exercising their kind offices to men, in relieving their wants, securing them from danger, and making their lives more comfortable.

> Myriads of spiritual beings walk the earth
> Unseen, or when we sleep, or when we wake.

Of them let us learn to rise in our affection to the great Father of all, aud thence descending, expand the heart from brother to brother, and to all mankind; of them let us learn never to be weary in the ways of well-doing, but to "mourn with them that mourn and to rejoice with them that do rejoice," until, having finished our work on earth, we shall be admitted to the temple above, not made with hands, eternal in the heavens.

THE FAREWELL,

TO THE BRETHREN OF ST. JAMES' LODGE, TARBOLTON.

Tune—"Good night, and joy be wi' you a'!"

I.

Adieu! a heart-warm fond adieu!
Dear brothers of the *mystic tie!*
Ye favor'd, ye *enlighten'd* few,
Companions of my social joy!
Tho' I to foreign lands must hie,
Pursuing Fortune's slipp'ry ba',
With melting heart, and brimfu' eye,
I'll mind you still, tho' far awa'.

II.

Oft have I met your social band,
And spent the cheerful, festive night;
Oft, honor'd with supreme command,
Presided o'er the *sons of light:*
And by that *hieroglyphic* bright,
Which none but *craftsmen* ever saw!
Strong mem'ry on my heart shall write
Those happy scenes when far awa'.

III.

May freedom, harmony, and love,
Unite us in the *grand design,*
Beneath th' omniscient eye above,
The glorious *Architect* divine?
That you may keep th' *unerring line,*
Still rising by the *plummet's law,*
Till *order* bright completely shine,
Shall be my pray'r when far awa',

IV.

And *you,* farewell! whose merits claim,
Justly, that *highest badge* to wear!
Heav'n bless your honor'd, noble name,
To *masonry* and *Scotia* dear!
A last request permit me here,
When yearly ye assemble a',
One *round,* I ask it with a *tear,*
To him, *the Bard that's far awa'.*

TESTIMONIALS.

From the Grand Lodge of Indiana.

The Committee to whom was referred the examination of 'THE CRAFTSMAN AND FREEMASON'S GUIDE, containing a delineation of the Rituals of Freemasonry, from the Degree of Entered Apprentice to that of Select Master and the Order of Priesthood,' beg leave to report—that they have given the same a careful examination, and find it, in their opinion, to be one of the best Masonic Manuals yet published. It possesses not only the recommendation of being as brief in its delineations as it is possible, in order to convey the necessary amount of masonic instruction, but it is entirely divested of those crude and imperfect historical digests of the Institution, with which most editors of masonic Text-books, have incumbered the literature of the Craft. This may be, by some, considered as a great omission, but in our opinion it is one demanded by the increasing light of masonic intelligence. The work merely professes to be a Freemason's Guide, and, in our opinion, to the practical Mason, it contains all the elements of a true directory. We not only take pleasure, therefore, in commending the present compilation, by Brother Cornelius Moore, to this Grand Lodge, and the brethren in Indiana, but to the fraternity at large, as, in the estimation of your committee, it is the most valuable compilation for practical purposes that has yet been presented to our consideration.

C. SCMIDLAPP,
D. P. HOLLOWAY,
LEWIS BURK."

From the Grand Lodge of Kentucky.

Resolved, That this Grand Lodge recommend to the Fraternity of Freemasons, the "CRAFTSMAN," by Bro. C. Moore, as a work of much merit, and a very excellent pocket companion, and of great utility in conferring degrees by the Lodges.

From the Grand Lodge of Ohio.

The Select Committee appointed to examine and report upon the merits of "THE CRAFTSMAN," a work compiled and arranged by Bro. CORNELIUS MOORE, and published by Bro. JACOB ERNST, at Cincinnati, having examined the same, report:—

That they find it to be judiciously arranged and in proper order—the language correct and expressive, the symbols rightly disposed, and the price so reasonable as to bring it within the reach of every Mason. The committee offer for adoption the following resolution:

Resolved, That the Grand Lodge of Ohio approve of the Craftsman, and recommend it to be used by the Lodges subordinate to this Grand Lodge.

Respectfully submitted,

WILLIAM FIELDING,
M. Z. KREIDER,
W. B. SMITH.

WASHINGTON, Hempstead Co., Ark., June 7th, 1850

I have to some extent carefully examined "THE CRAFTSMAN AND FREEMASON'S GUIDE," published by Bro. Jacob Ernst, of Cincinnati, Ohio, and observe with much pleasure and gratification its practical application. Its arrangement is excellent, and well calculated to facilitate greatly the explanation of the important lessons of the Order, easily directing the mind into a plain channel of masonic information. With these impressions I should rejoice to see its extended circulation, until it should be in the possession of every member of the craft in my own beloved Arkansas.

BENJ. P. JETT, P. G. M. of Ark.

ARKADELPHIA LODGE, NO. 19.

WHEREAS, Brother Samuel Reed has introduced to our notice a work entitled "THE CRAFTSMAN AND FREEMASON'S GUIDE," published by Brother Jacob Ernst, which has received a cursory examination, and meets the wishes and desires of the fraternity at this place;

Therefore be it Resolved, That we, believing it to be the very best working book which has come under our observation, most cordially recommend it to the favorable consideration of the craft.

Be it further Resolved, That the Compiler, Brother Moore, and Brother Jacob Ernst, the publisher, deserve the gratitude of the fraternity for presenting a work possessed of such advantages.

H. FLANAGIN,
W. M. BRICE,
JAS. H. OBAUGH, } Committee.

LITTLE ROCK, Ark., June 17th 1850.

On a careful examination of the "CRAFTSMAN," I give to it a most hearty approval, as the best working book I have seen. It is better arranged than Cross' Chart; and contains in addition to the matter of that Chart, that most valuable of all masonic writings, the ANCIENT CONSTITUTIONS. It is much superior in arrangement to the TRESTLE BOARD, and adheres more closely in its text to the approved standard works. E. H. ENGLISH.

THE TEMPLAR'S TEXT BOOK,---

Or Ritual of a Council of Knights of the Red Cross, and of an Encampment of Knights Templars, and Knights of Malta. Abridged from standard authors, by CORNELIUS MOORE, of Reed Encampment, No. 6, Ohio.

Morocco, marble edge, - - - - - - - - - 50
Morocco tuck, gilt edge, - - - - - - - - - - - - 75

DIPLOMAS,---

Beautifully engraved Master Masons' and Royal Arch Diplomas, 16 by 20 inches in size, on Paper and Parchment, for framing: also printed on bank note paper, and neatly put up in map form.

MASTER MASONS' AND ROYAL ARCH DIPLOMAS---

On Parchment, - - - - - - - - - - - - - 1 00
On Paper, Map form, - - - - - - - - - - - - 50

COUNCIL DIPLOMAS---

On Parchment, - - - - - - - - - - - - - 1 00
On Paper, Map Form, - - - - - - - - - - - 50

ENCAMPMENT DIPLOMAS---

On Parchment, - - - - - - - - - - - - - 1 50
On Paper, or Map from, - - - - - - - - - - - 75

www.ingramcontent.com/pod-product-compliance
Lightning Source LLC
LaVergne TN
LVHW020243110826
845151LV00003B/1017

* 9 7 8 1 4 2 5 5 2 9 3 1 4 *